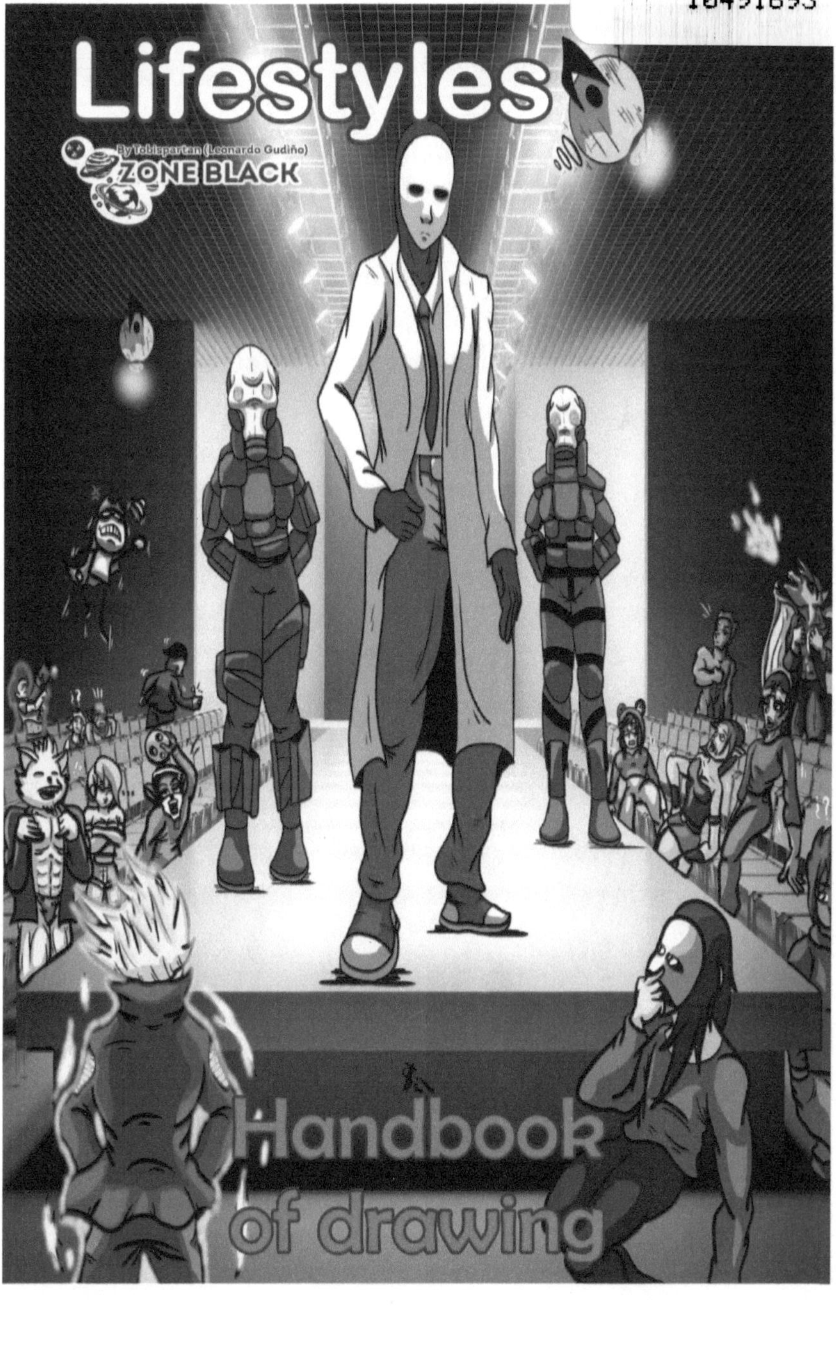

Lifestyles

By Tobispartan (Leonardo Gudiño)

ZONE BLACK

Handbook
of drawing

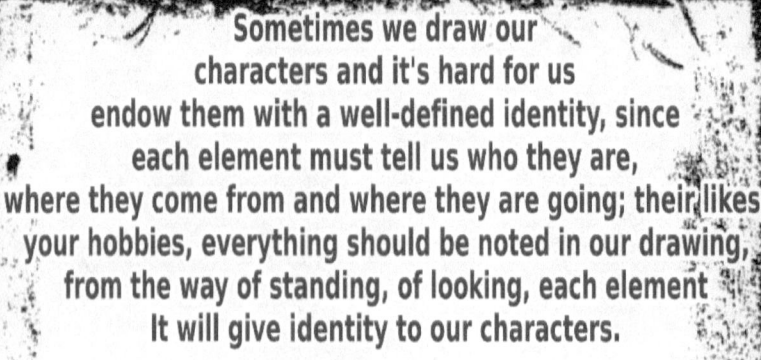

Sometimes we draw our
characters and it's hard for us
endow them with a well-defined identity, since
each element must tell us who they are,
where they come from and where they are going; their likes,
your hobbies, everything should be noted in our drawing,
from the way of standing, of looking, each element
It will give identity to our characters.

That is why this guide will analyze different styles
of life that occur in our current society.

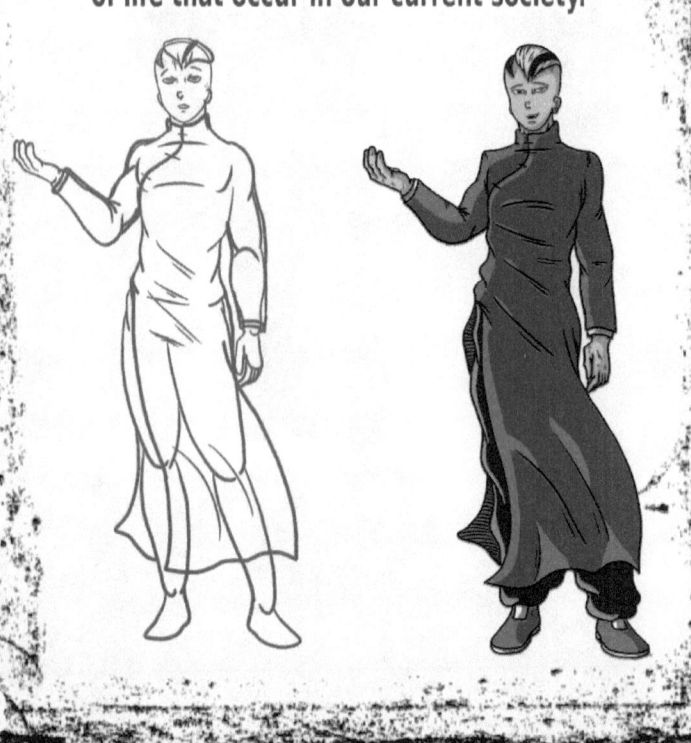

Hello to all new readers!

In this new drawing manual, we will learn
the new styles that today are
They are using, like Skates, Skatos,
the Emo (depressive), the Darketos, the Punketos,
Survivors, among others.

As I said earlier, this piece is for
learn from clothes that are used, to
the differences between some styles.

Keep in mind that all this will serve you
to be able to have variations in their drawings and
also in the clothes of his characters.

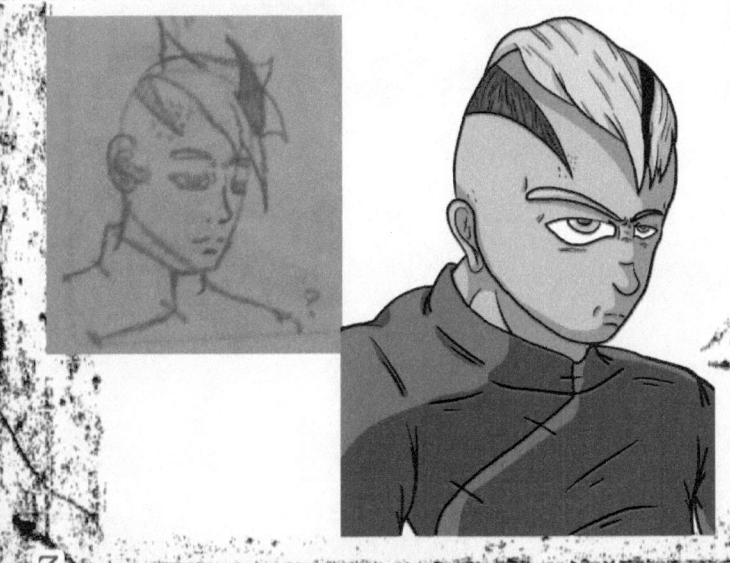

Skates

We will start with the young skates, which have a a bit extreme lifestyle, since they pass it between tubes, ramps, fractures and scrapes, anyway.

Note how the drawing shows indicate some things that almost they are never missing in the drawings skates, such as caps, bracelets, rings, logos in the shirts that always are useful, since with them you can see that it really is a skateboard and not a simple hobbyist.

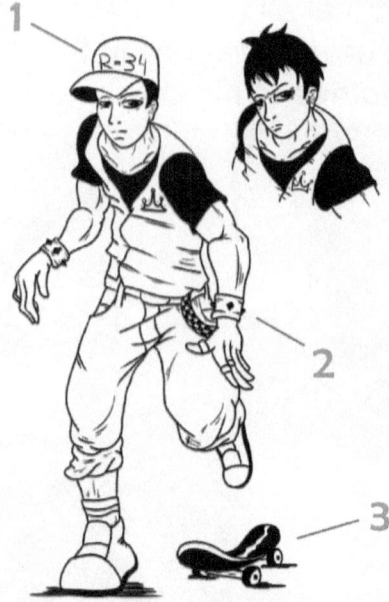

1. Logos
2. Accessories (bracelets).
3. The big tennis shoes and skateboard.

Well now we move on to the skate girls, as
is almost the same, but remember that not all
girls are skateboard lovers. This time he
we have added one (indicated at number 1),
but note that the cap, the sweatshirts and others
garments can be seen with the naked eye. Other
accessory that can not be missing in skates are the
belts or ribbons that go down the side
of the leg.

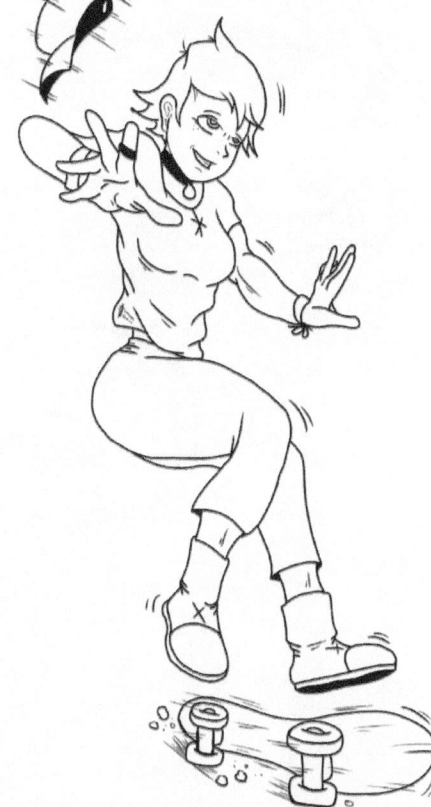

In this other drawing we can see the cap and the sweatshirt, seen in profile and from the front, which of course They are from a skateboard, since usually they all have caps or sweatshirts with caps (something to cover head).

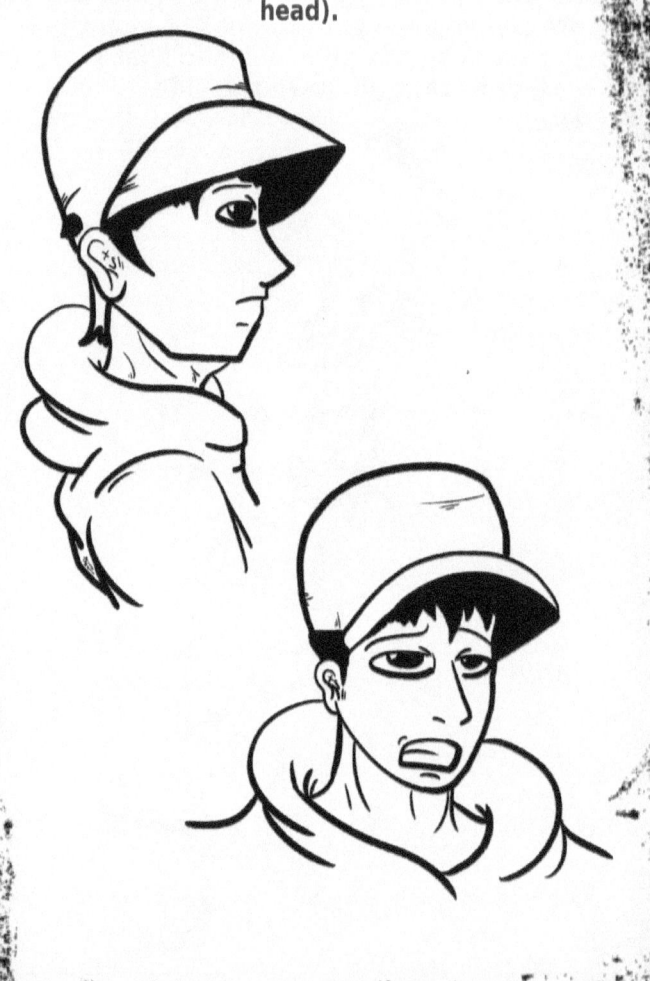

The girl here shows her jacket that,
Unlike the others, it does not have a logo, but that
It does not mean that it is a skateboard, since they also use
Bermuda shorts (1) and headbands (2), plus
if it's a girl.
The tennis shoes are great (3 boots).

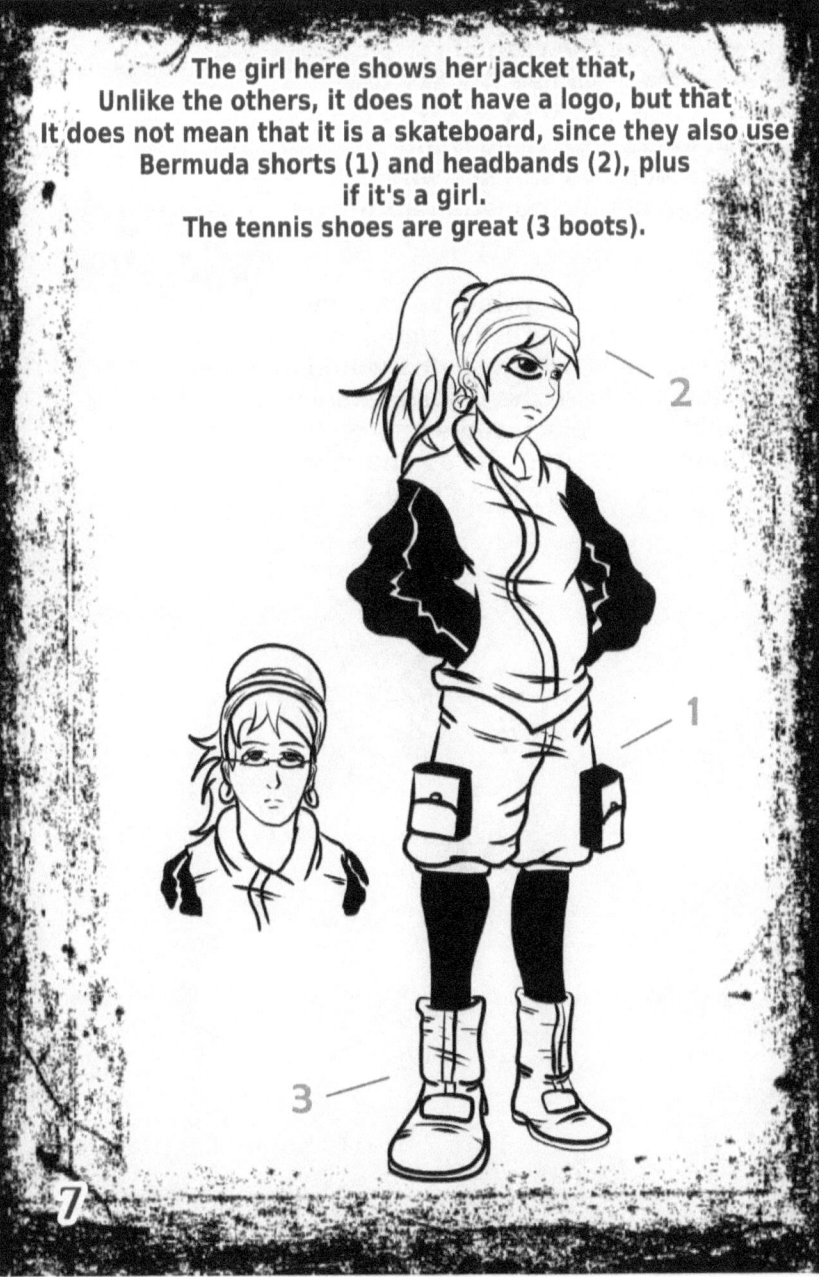

Now we have the case of
skatos. Many people will say that
is the same, but they are wrong, since the
These logos tend to be from
music groups up patches with
signs against the government of your
country.

Skatos

In the following drawing we can find
in number 1 the aerosols, which they use to
paint the walls, which skates would never do.
The number 2 are the logos as above
We said it and black and white plaid T-shirts.
In number 3 are the gloves and face masks, the
pants must be very large below.

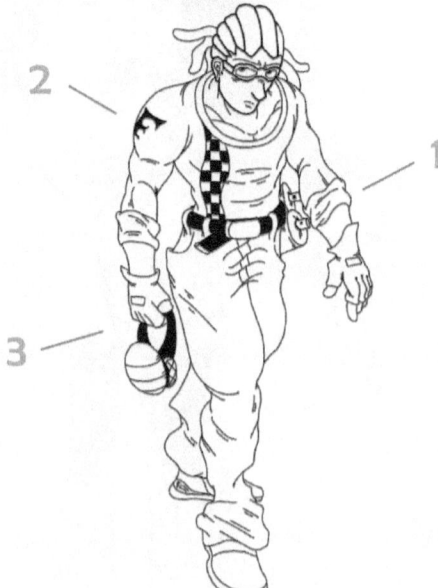

2

1

3

NOTE: Some use Glasses

The hairstyles could also be very different with each other, which skateboarders wouldn't mind, but the skatos yes. Now some also wear the shirts with three-quarter sleeves and vests. Not for being skatos means that they cannot wear pants, but pants it has to be big from the bottom.

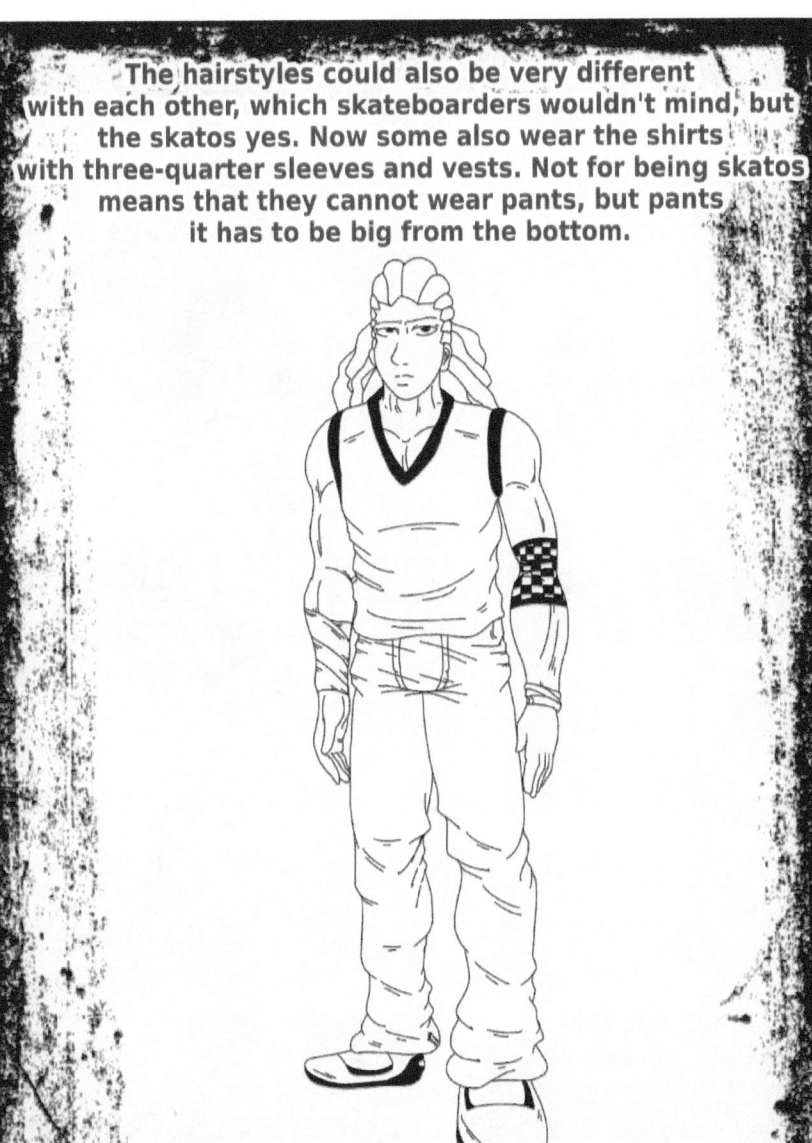

We continue with the skatos. Many of them, not being able, bring a spray so easily mind, opt for the down ones.

In the character of this page we can see how it brings other types of gloves, very different from the first skato. By the brightness and textures of this one we could say that are made of leather.

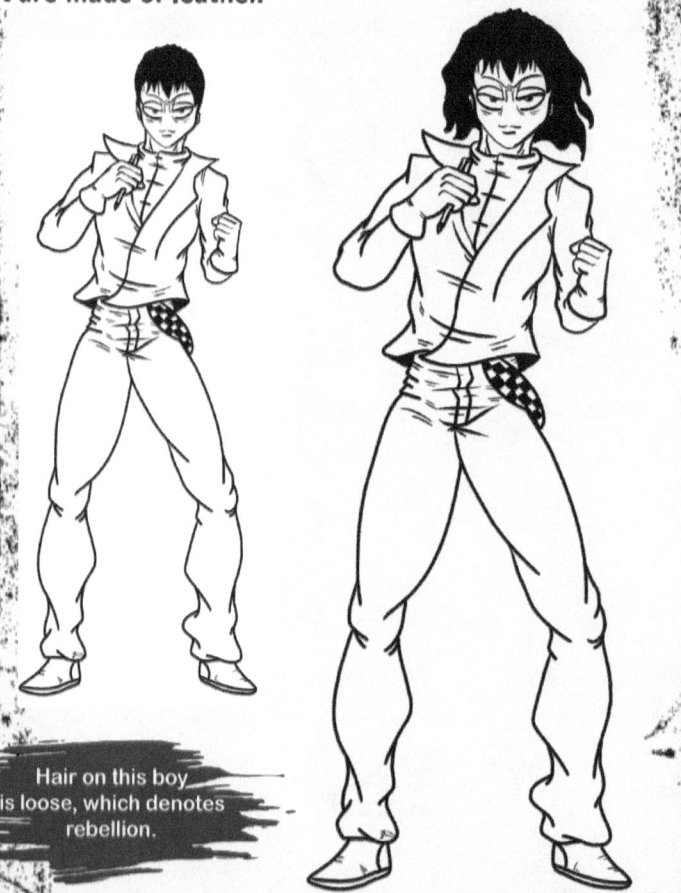

Hair on this boy is loose, which denotes rebellion.

Well now we will start with another lifestyle.
For those hip hop lovers, here are the
hopers, characters to whom we must dress them with
pants to jeans. We have a
girl dressed in pants, but to differentiate herself
of another style he brings very high, very big tennis shoes,
gloves showing rudeness, since the
hip hop is like that, and by the features we could say
which is black skin.

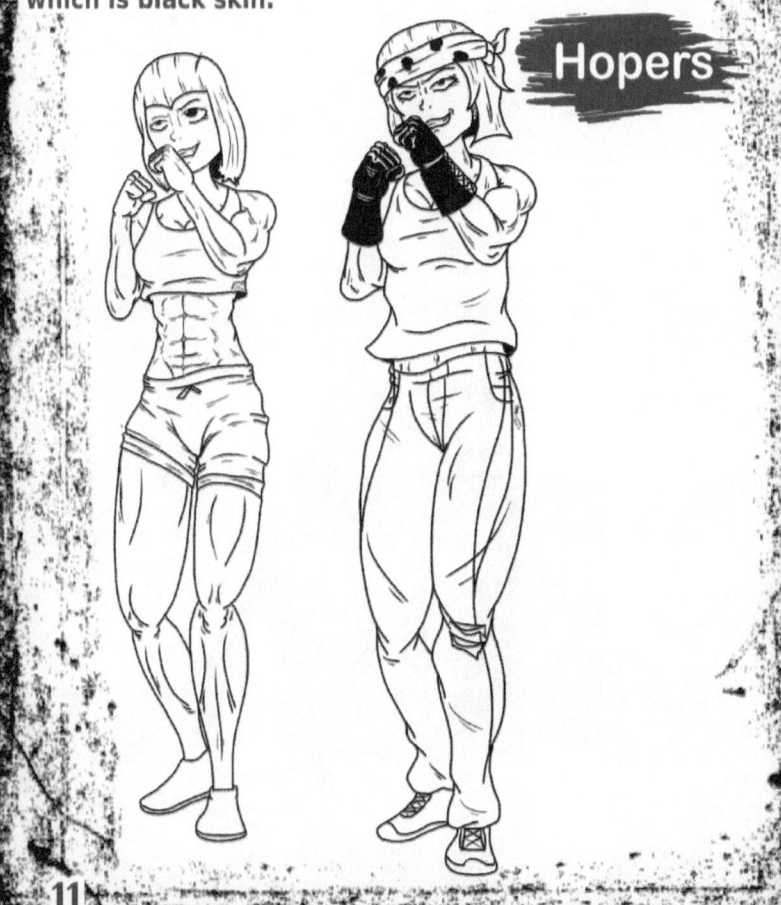

Hopers

Remembering Skates, in this case we dress different, with a goose down jacket (2), very common in hopers, full pants, high-top and pitch-black sneakers (3), the headband does not is so tight (1) and the cap on the jacket is too great, since hopers wear very baggy clothes.

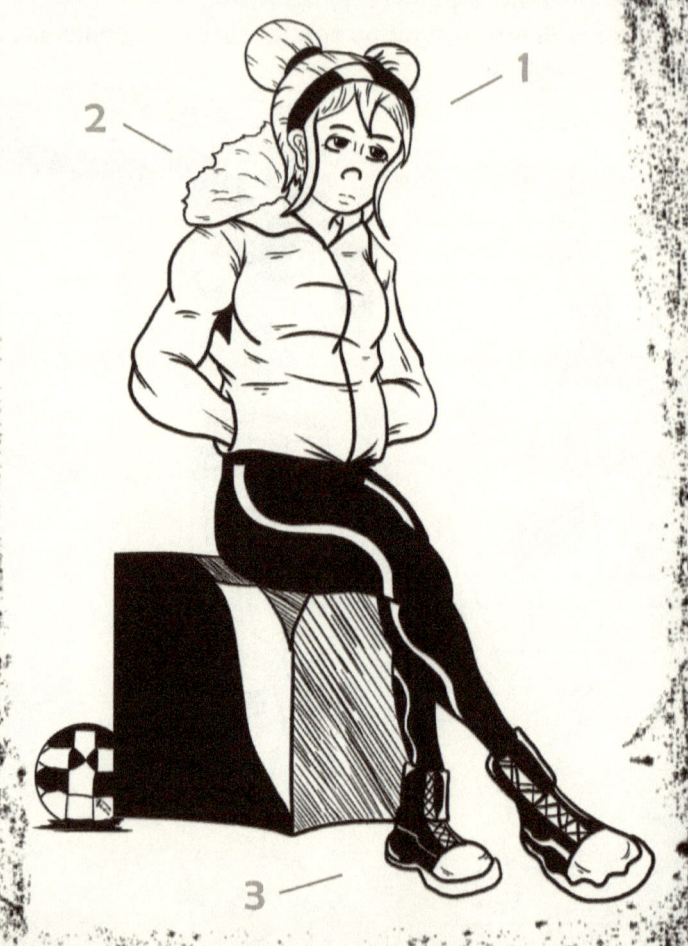

2

1

3

In the same way this girl, previously with
skate clothes, and now wearing hoper clothes.
Unlike skates, she wears a hat for the cold,
he even brings some little pompoms.
The hoodie cap is gone and so is
the tape on the side of the leg.

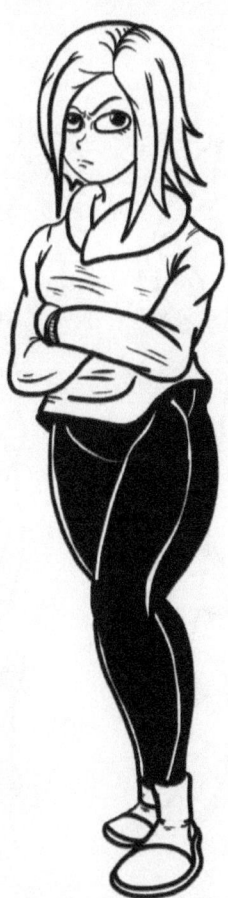

Now we will see how the boys hopers are very different
girls, since they wear caps or bandanas (A);
some also use jackets or t-shirts, and not
wrist straps may be missing.

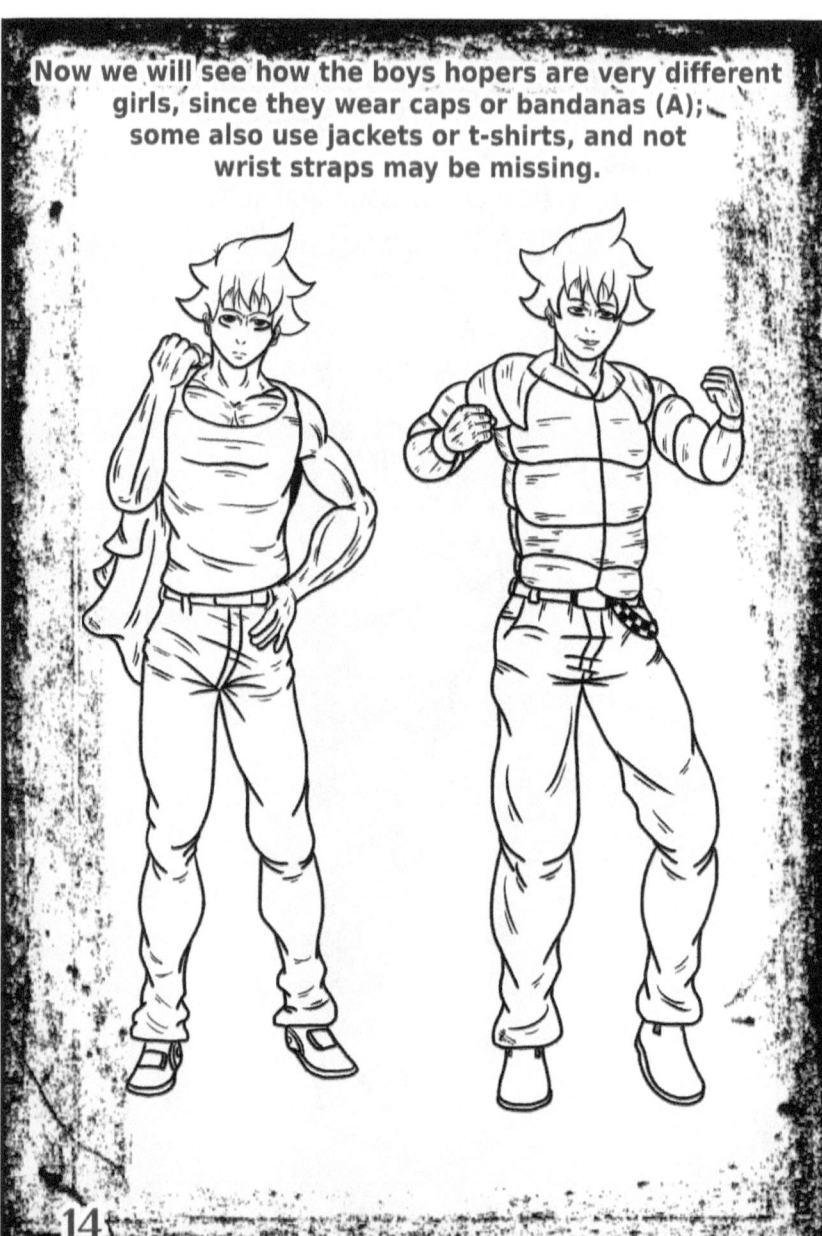

Many of the hopers wear baseball jerseys, like the first drawing; and others, special t-shirts, of course, with engraved initials. One or the other uses bandana and the cap at the same time, each one his taste, Of course.

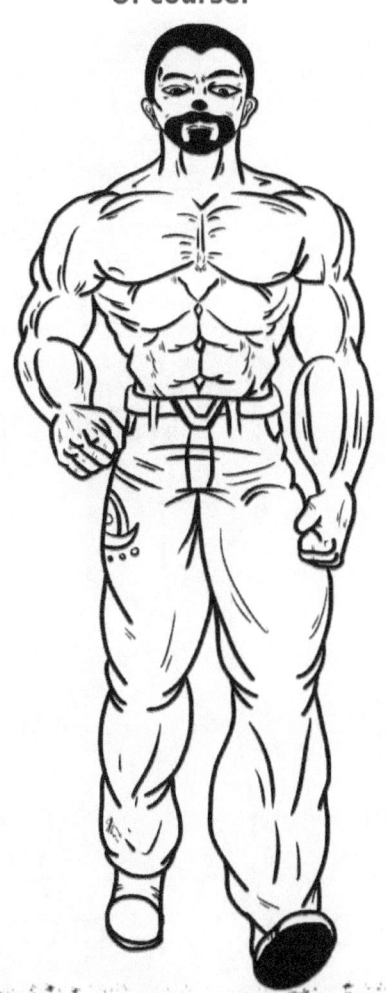

Many of them have tattoos on their skin, from names of anything in English, even very rare figures. Another characteristic is that his haircut is very short or with braids.

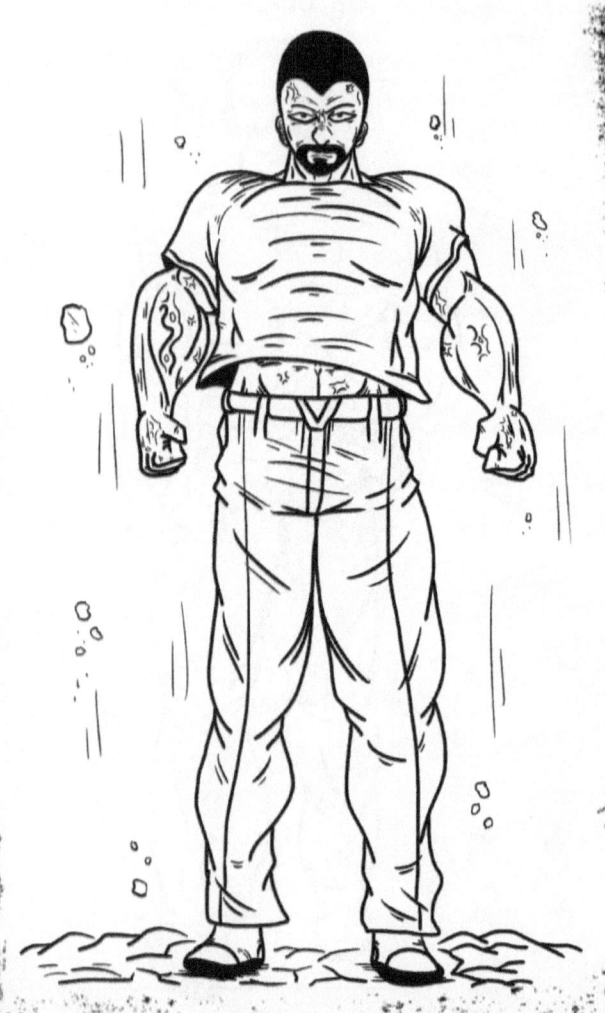

Well tired of hopers, we couldn't shut out
to the famous strawberries (or rich men). Many guys and
girls are strawberries, or basically anyone who
boast of high economy (even if you don't really have it),
nowadays they are the ones that abound in all cities,
but good.

First of all, a strawberry is very different from
above, as he tries to dress well in front of the girls
more than anything, or before the boys.

We will start with the man. The hairstyle must be rebellious
not very modern, some wear the shirts loose,
clear (1), dress pants or denim, shoes
They must be fashionable, like this guy.

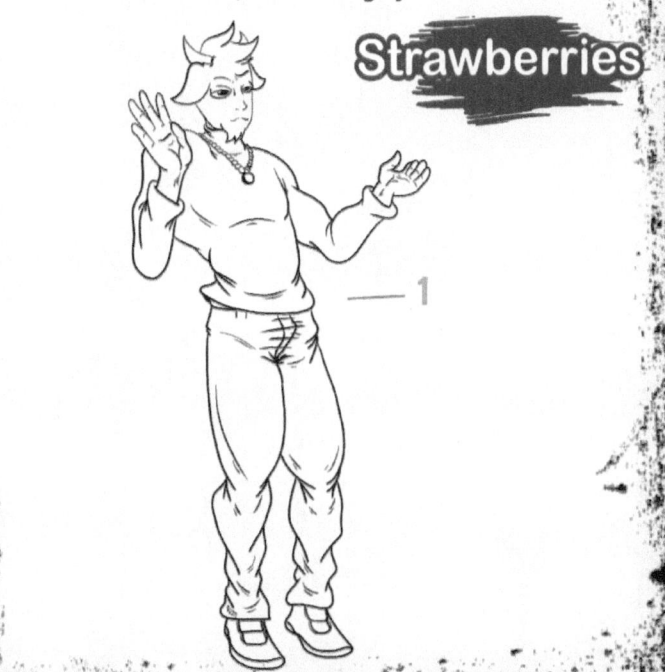

Strawberries

—1

Now there are the girls. They wear miniskirts or
short dresses, for the boys to notice them,
shoes or heels (2), and jackets or coats (1)
they are very important in a girl truly
luxurious, not to mention the hairstyles, which must be very
"Fashion".

1

2

Many girls wear glasses. The strange thing is that I hardly know They put them on and they only bring them on their heads. They are also used the famous low-cut blouses, and miniskirts like we previously said it. The lips must be painted just like the eyes.

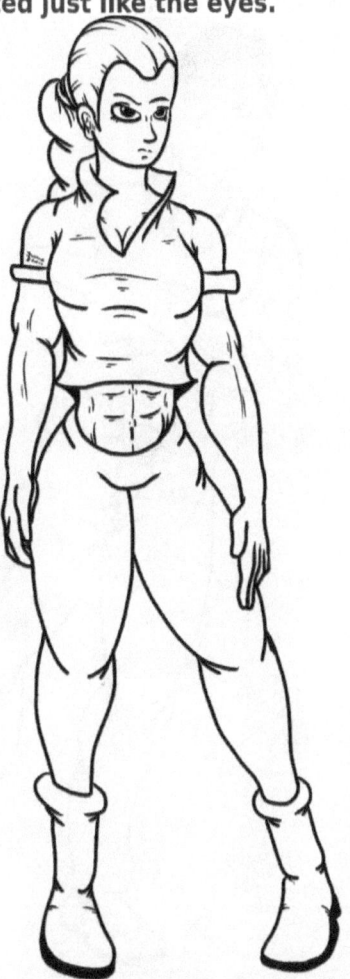

Boys wear blue jeans, sure, always
with a very simple belt. This type of persons
You could use the vests with casual shirts. Never
their watch will be missing; and in some, headbands
to be able to stop the hair.

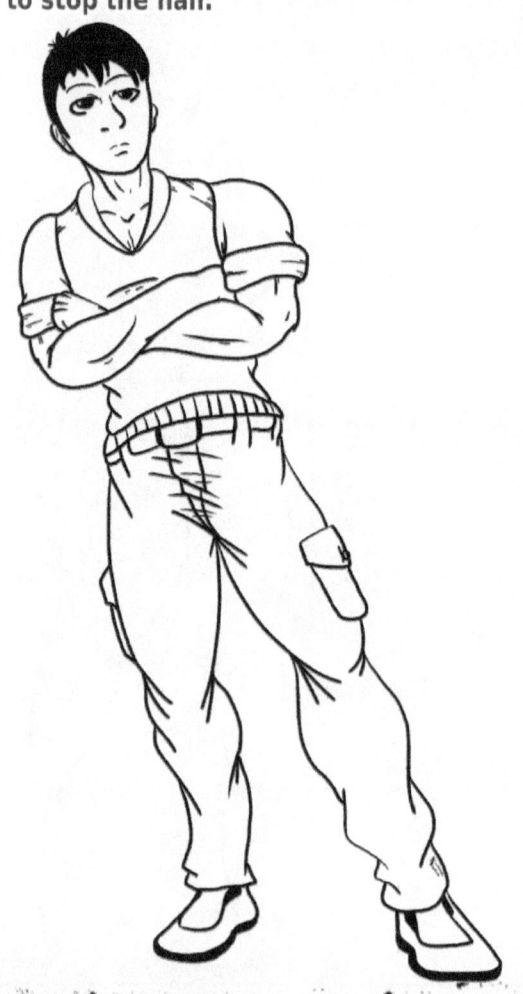

But not because of the above we can deprive them of the pants.
They can use them, but only if they are of some brand in
special. Sweatshirts can also be worn, but
note the difference between skate and strawberry. This one, for
In general, it is always very aesthetic both the man and
the woman.

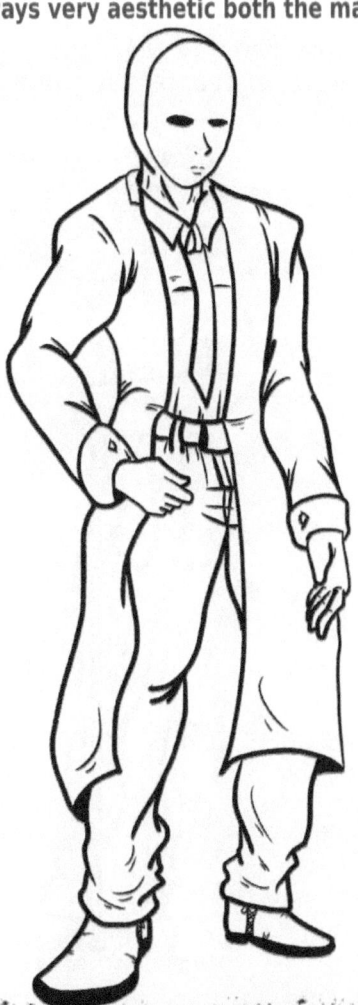

Like man, girls can also wear
sweaters, sweatshirts, full pants, etc. The
only condition is the same as men's, and
never lose style.

Hair can be loose like this girl, lips
very well painted, of course, the same color as the pants.

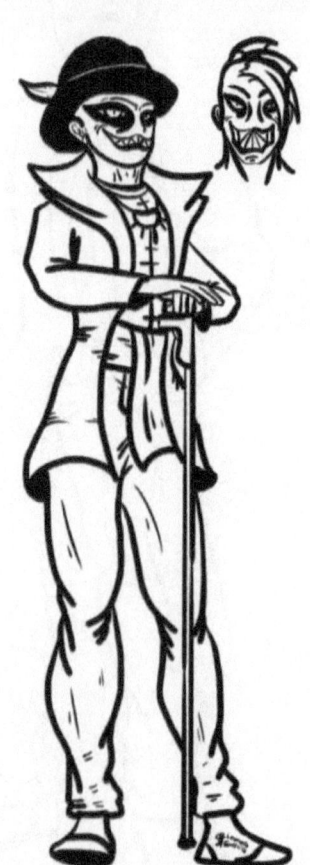

In boys, shirts will never be missing and much less if they are very tight. These may have logos, but not as grotesque and dirty as skates. These logos are more aesthetic and detailed. Bracelets they are also very important. And see that this boy yes he exercises.

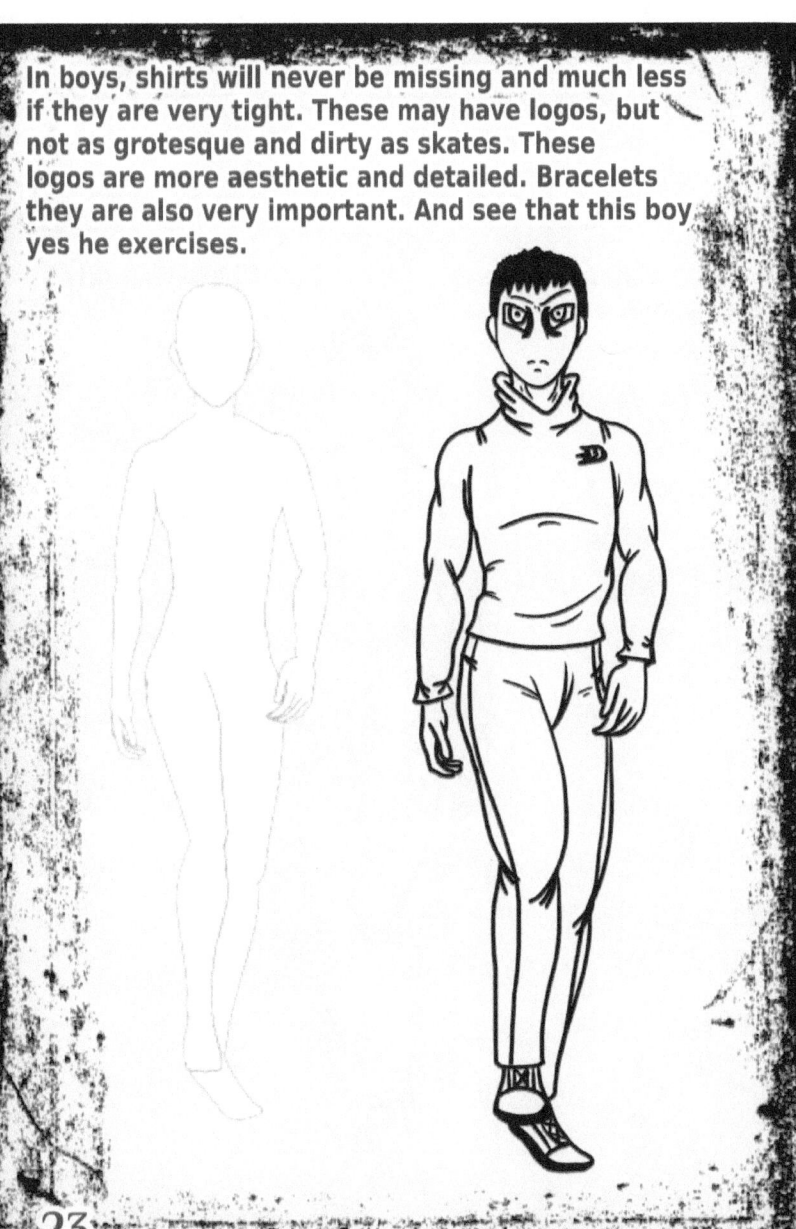

Now we draw the same guy, only this time he brings a raincoat (1). But we took off his sleeves to give you a look of youth and rebellion. Strawberries they also have their rebellion, but calmer than the previous types of life.

Note: By adding the cell phone we could say that it is a strawberry very Junior.

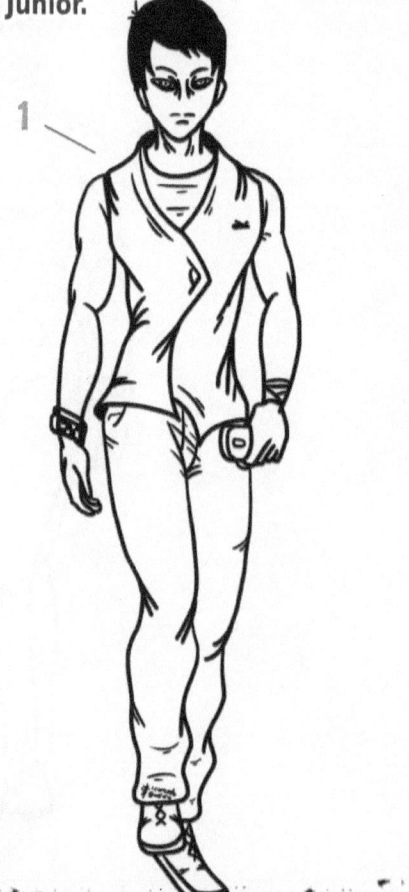

1

Well, as we said earlier, you could use sport shirts, also the bracelets which in this case are Leather. The pants, apparently, are denim and by the type of bags is defined as being very sporty.

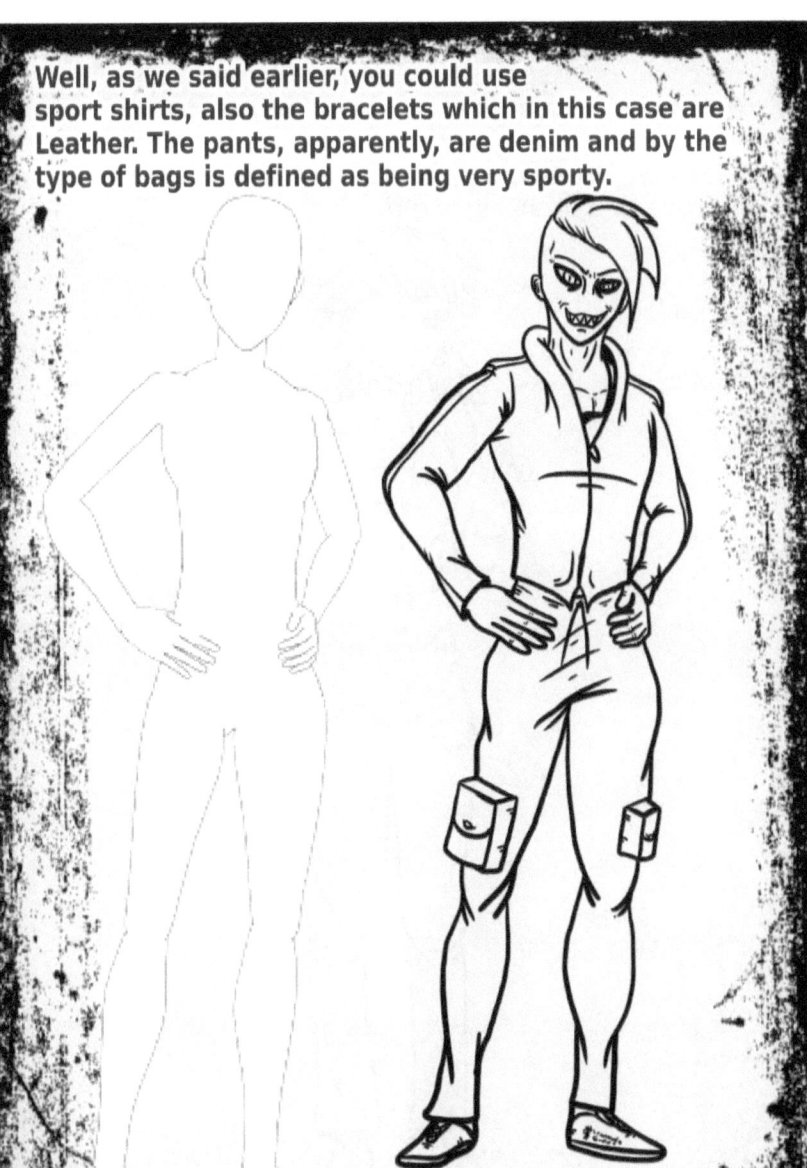

Girls could wear spandex pants and blouses very short that attract a lot of attention from a boy. The dark glasses are very necessary in case of the presence of the sun. The slippers will never be missing in the wardrobe of a strawberry girl.

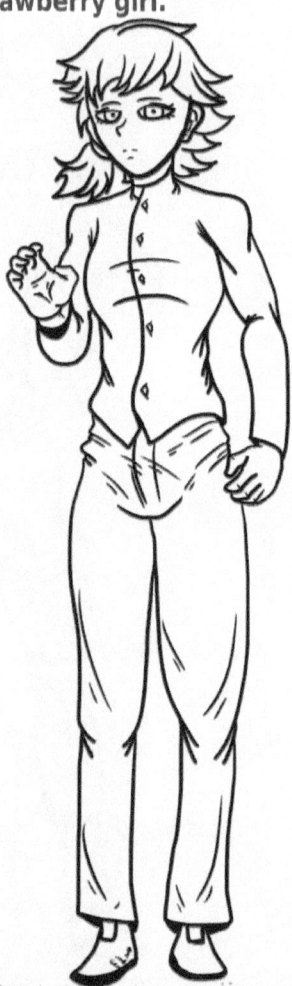

The strawberry guy also usually wears the famous shirts turtleneck, like very tight jackets;
and pants, plain or striped; the shoes not to mention,
Of course, the time of laces is over.

The boy's hairstyle must be short in order to show off the turtleneck, otherwise it wouldn't be noticeable.

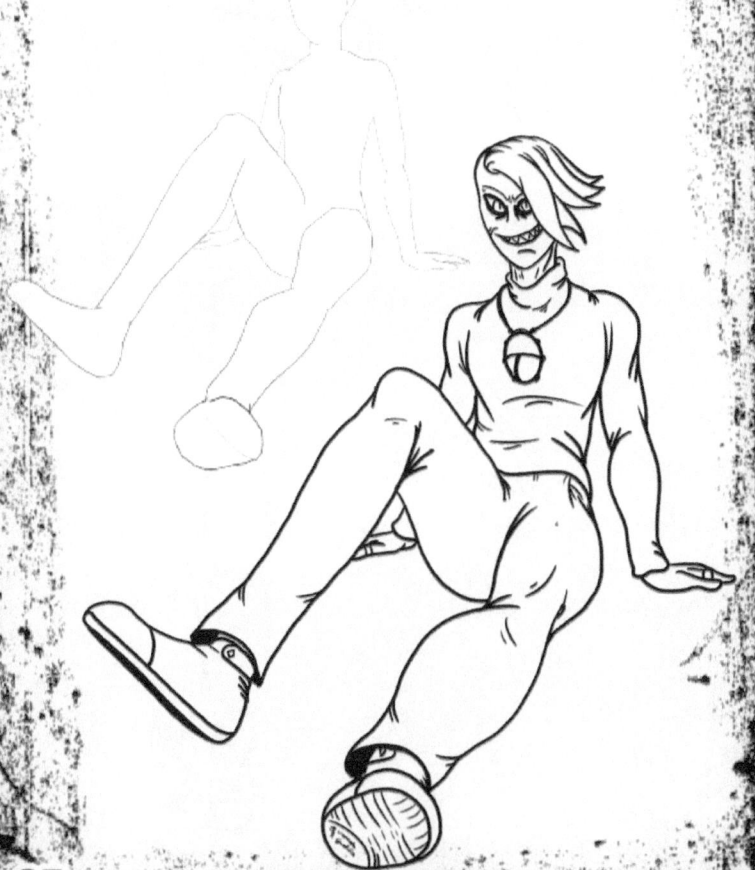

Like women, men too they have the right to wear sunglasses. Here we have placed you a sweater for the cold seasons. The shoes are now casual, the hairstyle is a bit rebellious and longer than that of the previous character.

Now after studying the rebellious boys, like
the skatos, the skates, the hopers and the strawberries,
it is his turn turn to the nerds (scholars or scholars),
since they have an important role in comics or plays.

In all the stories there are a few children
they are called clumsy, but not stupid, since they are
too smart.

In this case we have the before and after, of course
it is not to see how I change, but to see the difference
between the nerd and the others. Nerds wear glasses,
hairstyles are very serious and they usually wear shirts
and vests with diamonds, quite the opposite of the
character on the right since the other's hairstyle is
modern, and the shirt and the band "micro-por"

on the nose they give a kind of
rebellion, a fact that is not typical of a
nerdy boy.

Nerds

We have the case of this girl, who being studious earns the title of nerd. For the simple fact of using glasses and the little tie, and also for having in the hand the pencil, we can say that she is a very dedicated.

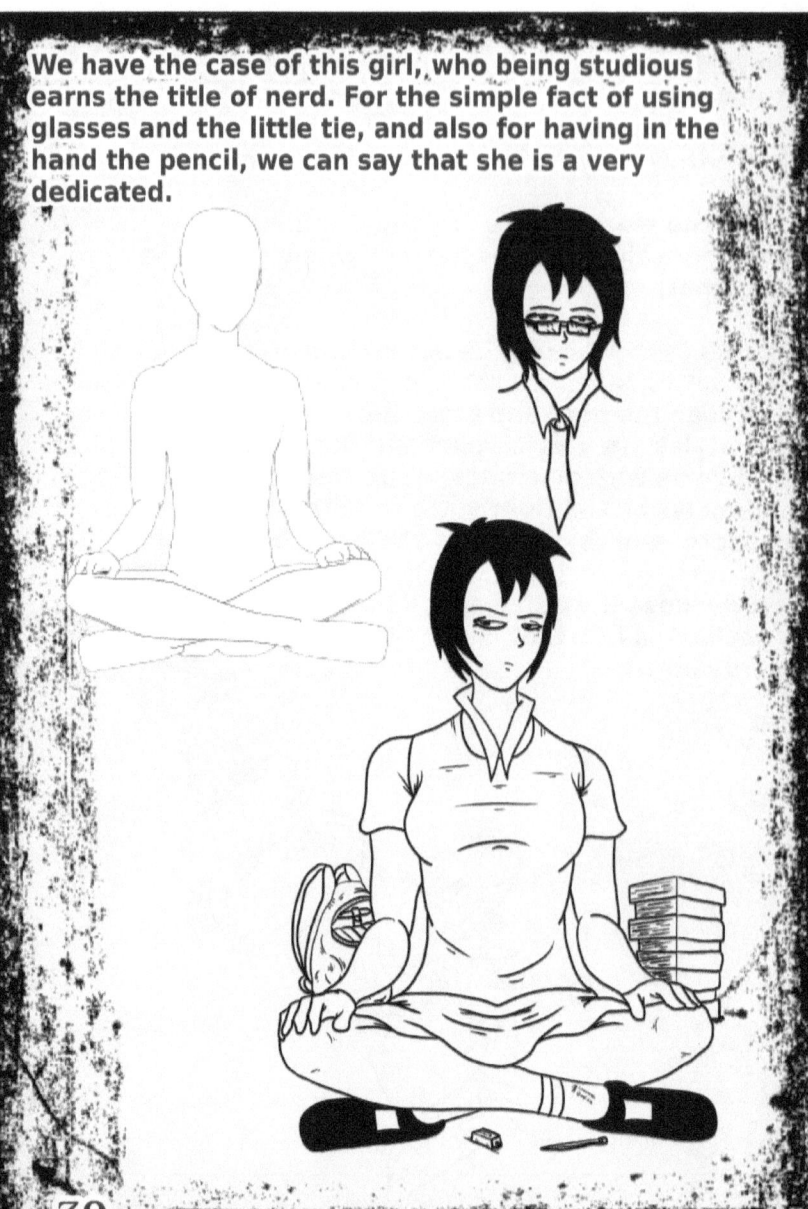

Now we have the same girl, only this time
we have placed some accessories that you should bring
all the nerds in the world, like backpacks (1),
pencils (2) and what cannot be missing in the hands of the boys
nerds: notebooks (3). These are the accessories that are not
they may be missing in a nerd room.

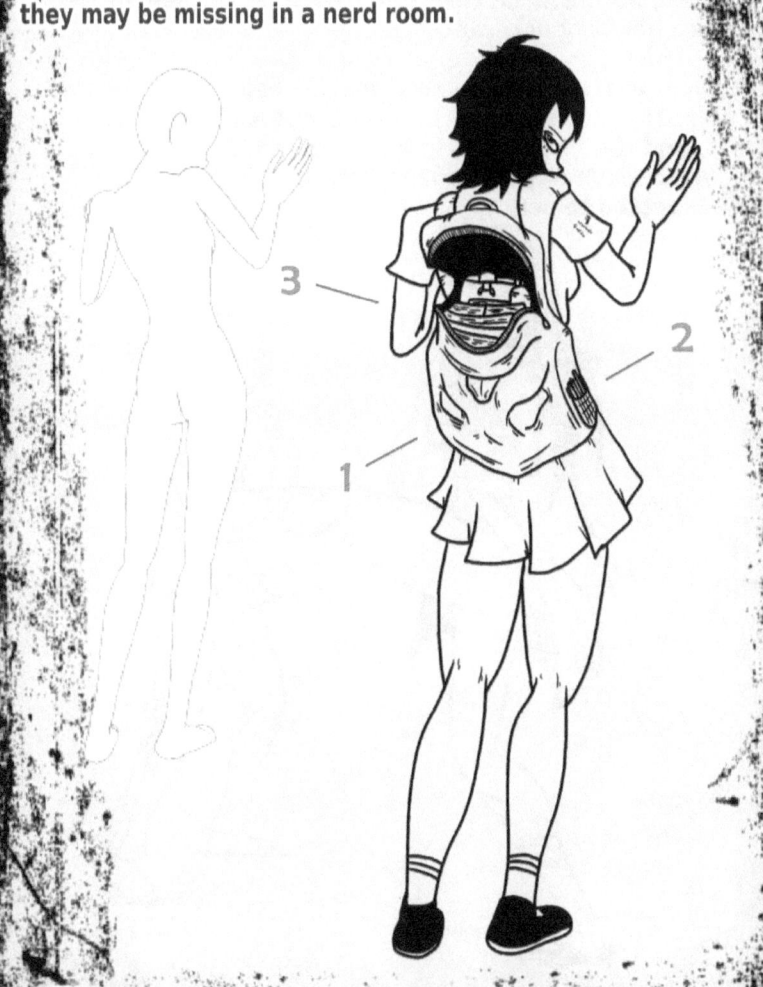

In these two girls we have placed different clothes
of clothes, but this does not mean that they are different,
since by the simple fact of wearing large glasses and having
an older hairstyle means that the person is
very shy and does not like to be very sociable to say,
of course, not because they don't want to, but because
they are not very accepted.

But nerds exercise too, even if they're bad
for this. That's why the girl on the right is wearing a
pants, and the one on the left a bermuda. Of course
will never teach beyond what many of you
they expected to see.

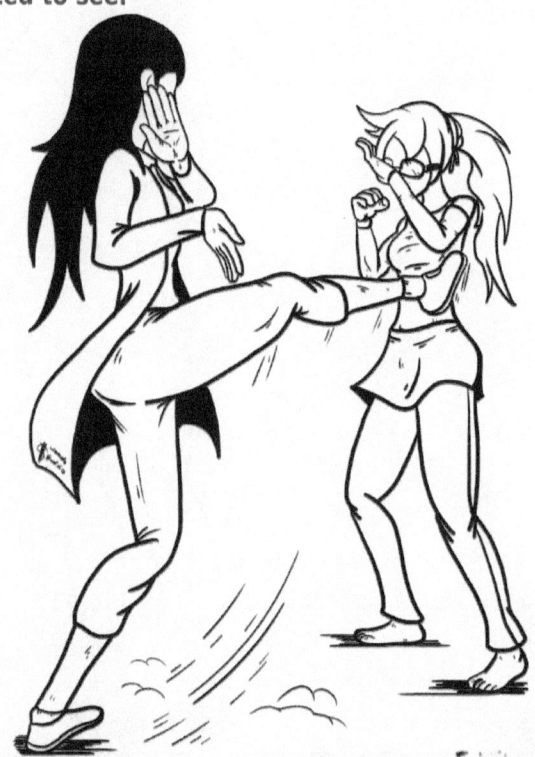

This guy is very intellectual, but he's still nerdy because of many features that can be seen with the naked eye. One of them is the buttons on the belt of his backpack, the tight pants and other features that could be the T-shirt with thick-framed collar and glasses.

Note: The bigger the backpack means that it carries too many tools.

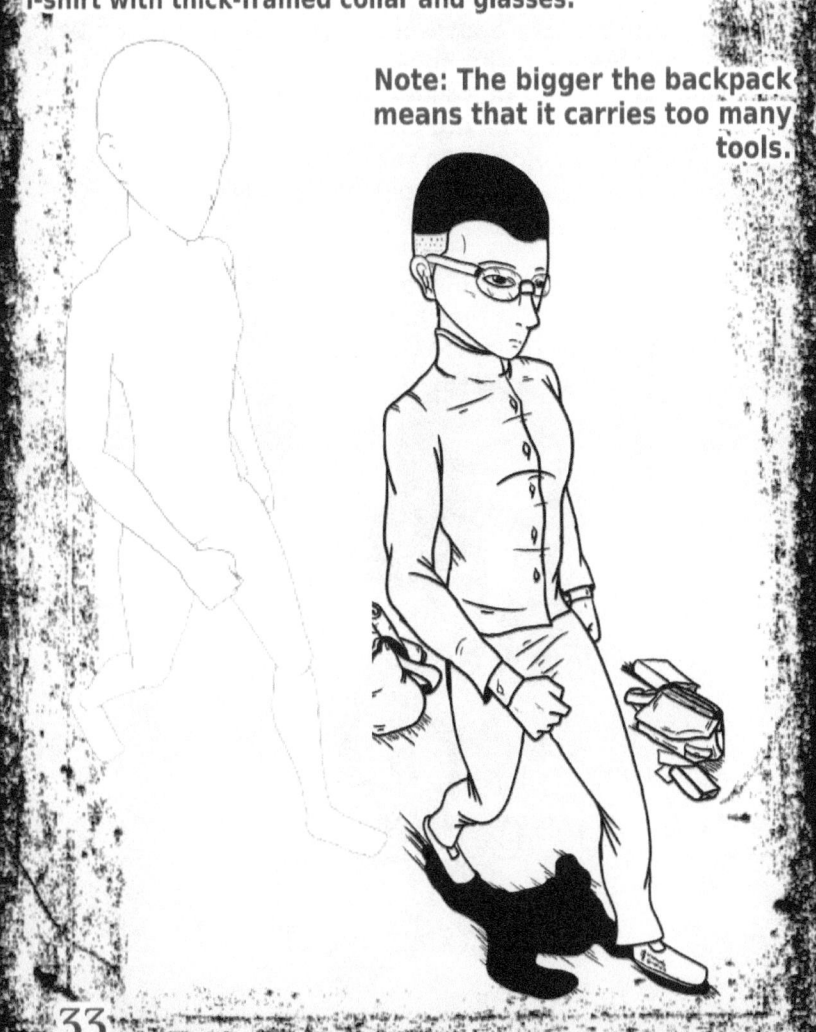

We say goodbye to classes and grades
approving, and we go with the evil ones, with the
dark, because we have to explain the clothing of the
darks and how to make a character dark.

To be able to make a character dark is very simple.
In this case we have the cute girl dressed in black,
but it is not enough to make it look dark. Anyway,
First of all, the blacker the clothes is a lot
best. What am I going with that? What I want to say is
no garment should have a color other than red,
black and purple.

Note: Some clothes have colors like white, or Blue,
but white or blue is sometimes accepted,
depending on the character drawn.

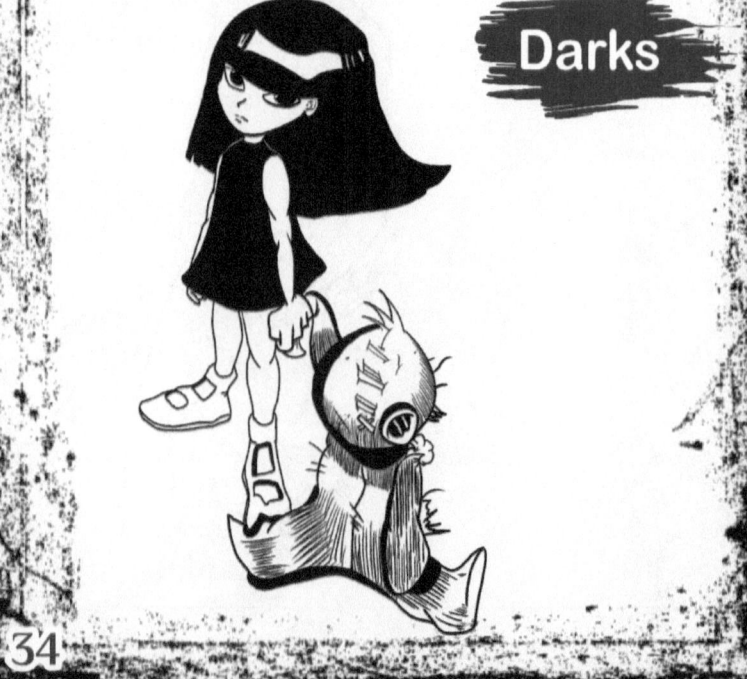

Darks

The same girl is still not so dark. We will add a macabre scenario, or maybe it isn't, but the fact having crosses and a moon denotes darkness and evil.

Many brand these people as satanic, but that's a lie. Many are darks just for fun and to hide your feelings a bit.

Well, we already put the bottom, now we put more objects to darken and make our character.

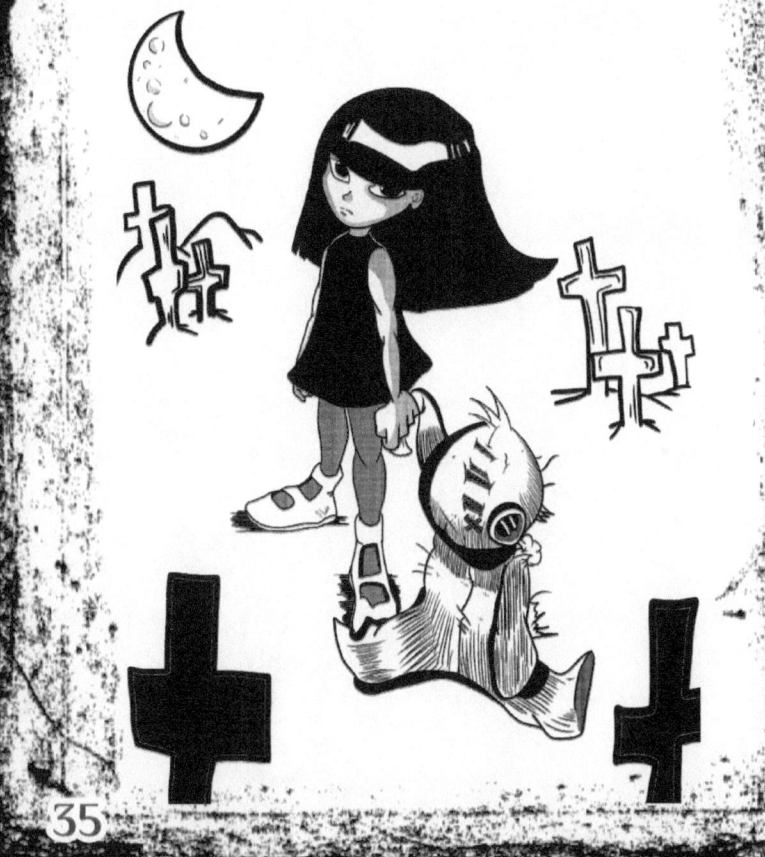

35

The girl now looks more macabre with that bear, everything broken and with the scene much darker. The objects and backgrounds often give another aspect to characters, for example, if you draw a nerd it is necessary put it in your room studying or in a library, likewise with the darks placing them in places mostly old, neglected or abandoned preferably at night, since bandalos like skatos can also be in places abandoned to graffiti but during the day.

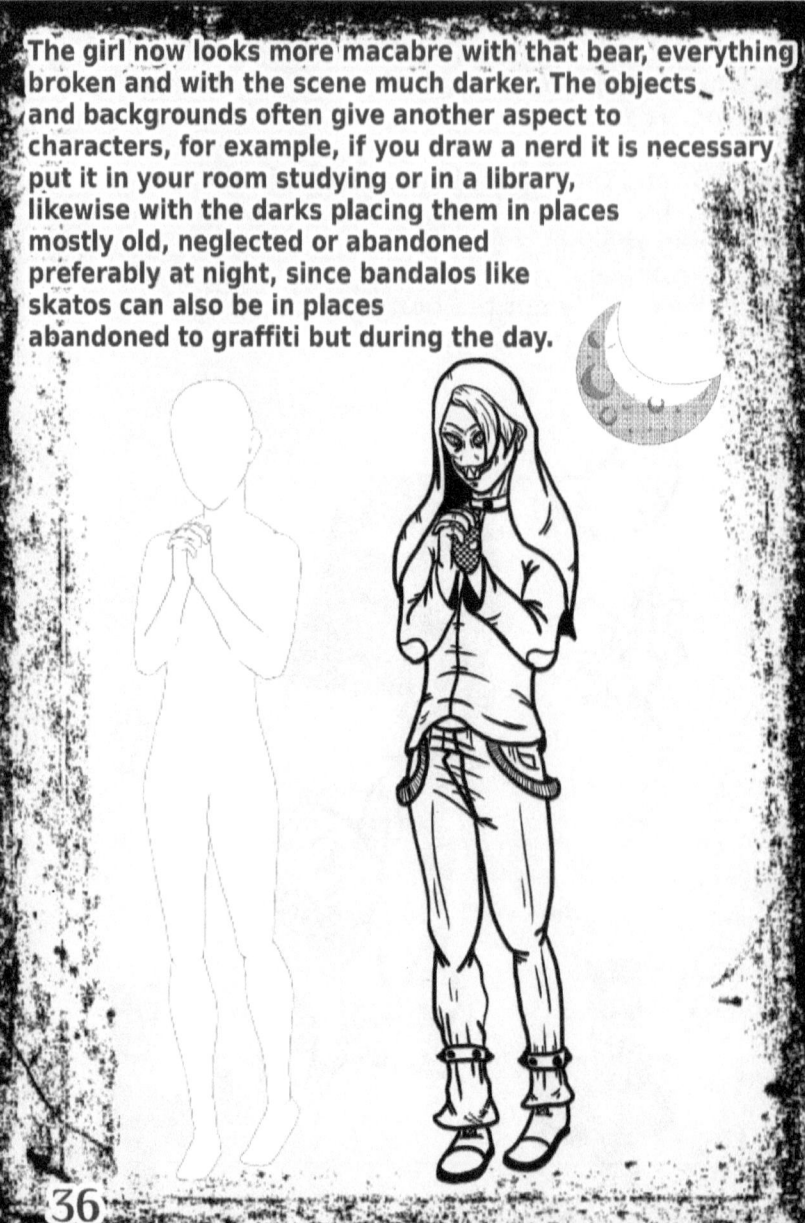

We continue with them. Trench coats are very useful in these characters, and many of them have long hair covering part of his face. The pants are black and the shoes have to have a bigger sole than the same shoe.

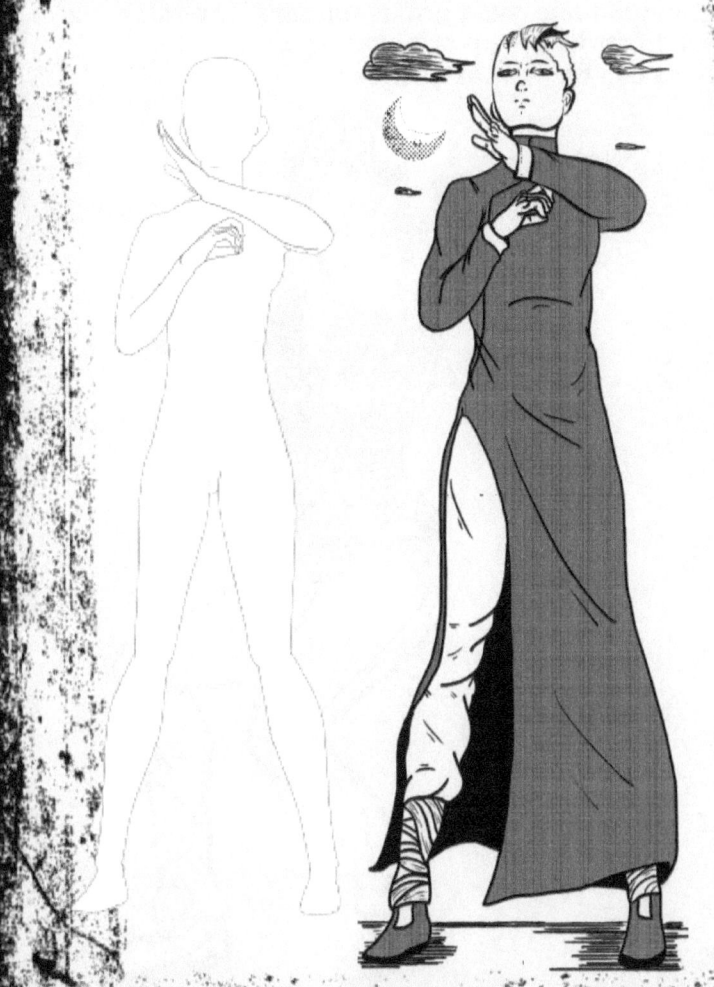

Many darks wear fur jackets. To be able to draw
leather clothes should be made small white lines
as reflections in the folds of clothing, as shown
in this guy's jacket.

Sure, painted nails could not be missing. The colors more
Common in darks are black and deep purple.
Hairstyles can be a bit extravagant.

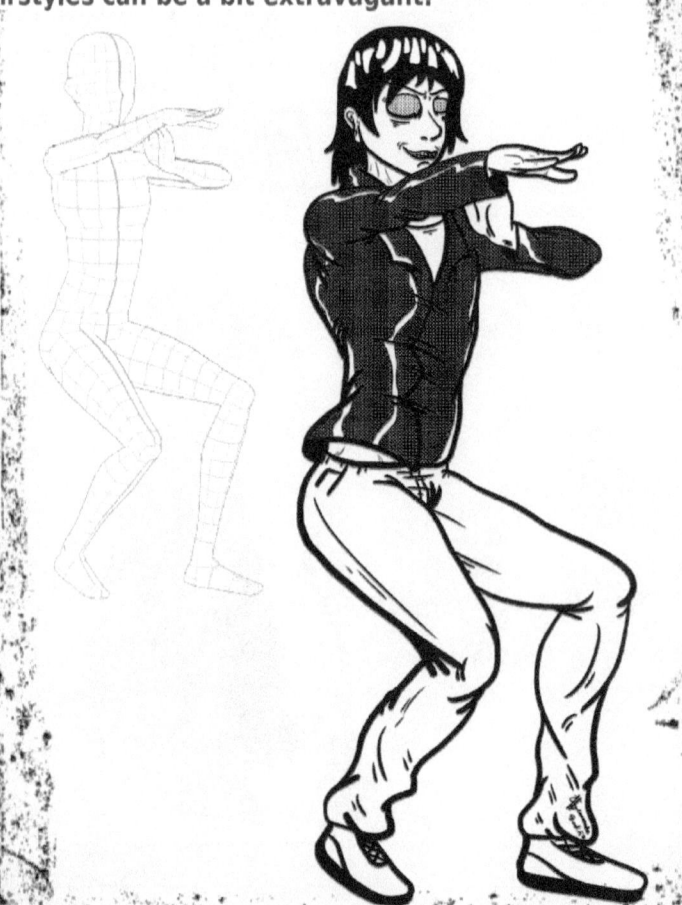

Many of these guys wear fishnet tops, which are very transparent. Again the hairstyles are very important, some of them get painted hair of purple, red and gray tones.

The pants can also be canvas. Many times we have seen these pants and we wonder what You feel rays when it's too hot, don't you think? Anyway, this type of pants is full of light reflections as shown in drawing (A).

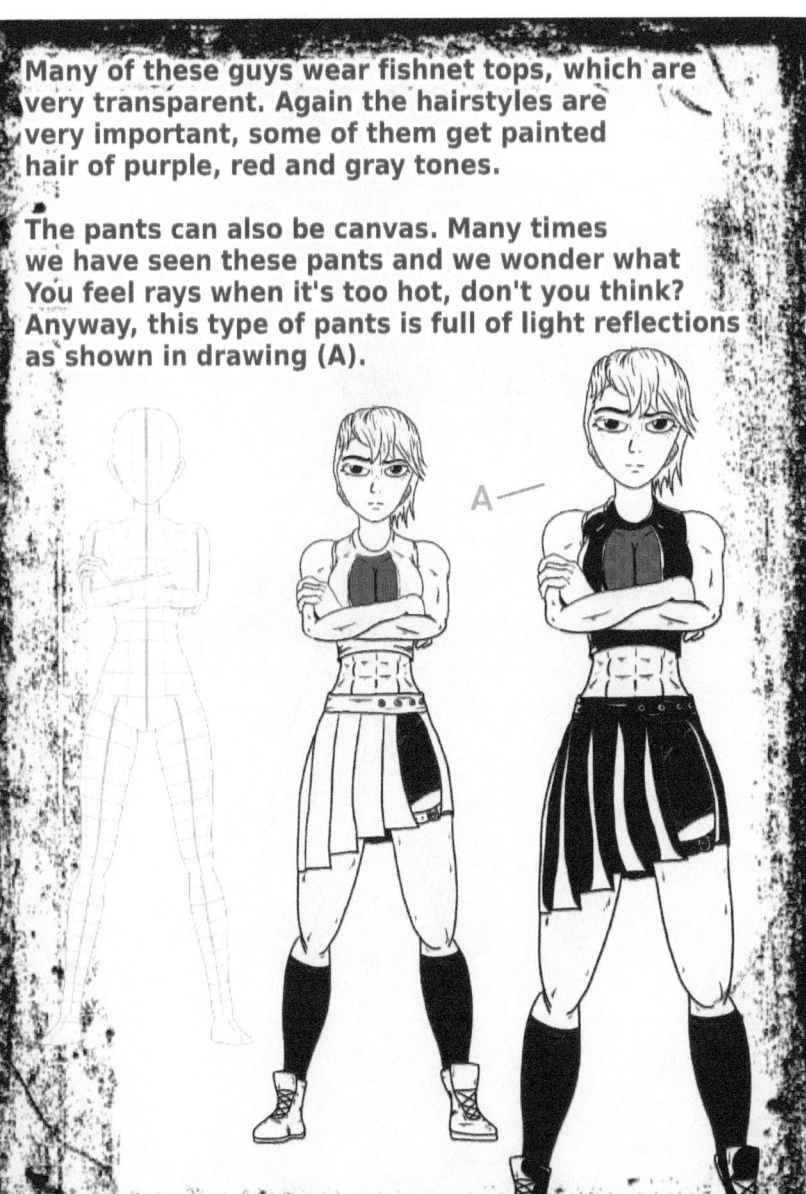

A—

Many of these guys wear fishnet tops, which are
very transparent. Again the hairstyles are
very important, some of them get painted
hair of purple, red and gray tones.

The pants can also be canvas. Many times
we have seen these pants and we wonder what
You feel rays when it's too hot, don't you think?
Anyway, this type of pants is full of light reflections
as shown in drawing (A).

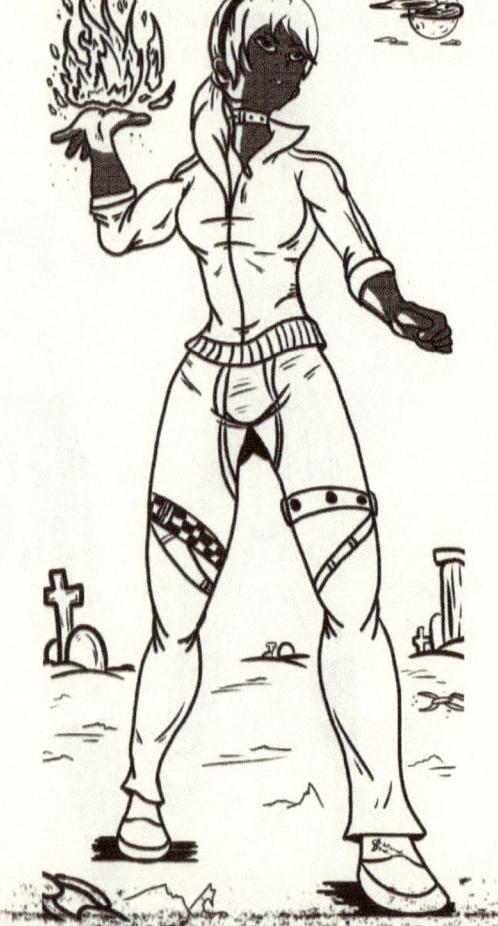

Finally we have some accessories that
Normally darks boys wear, like belts
neck, spike bracelets, screws,
nails, etc. The belts must be very large,
contrary to the strawberry boys. Some boots they
wear bring the famous bushings, and the big studs too
are important.

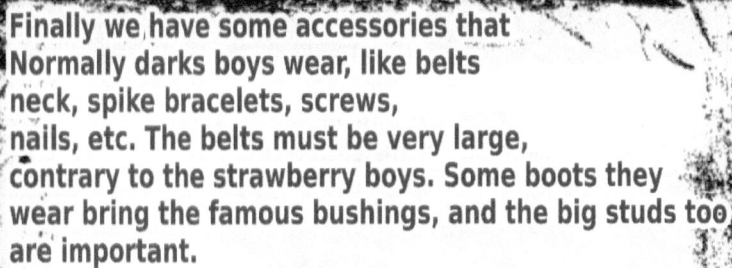

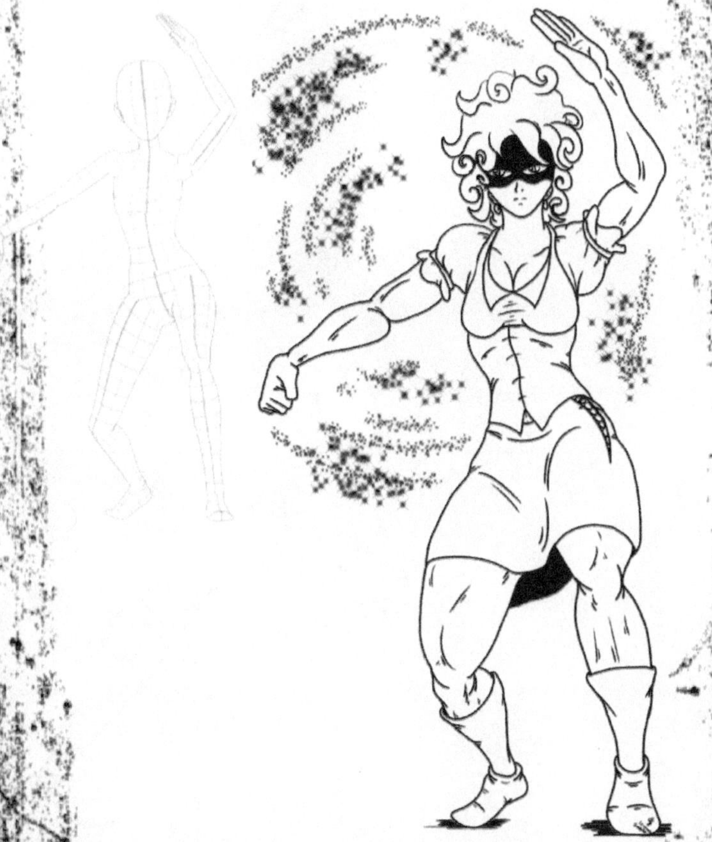

Well, we have the same girl above, but this time she
we have placed a cape to give it a vampire look.

Another thing we forgot to mention is that
rings are very important in girls, in men
it's just the bracelets.

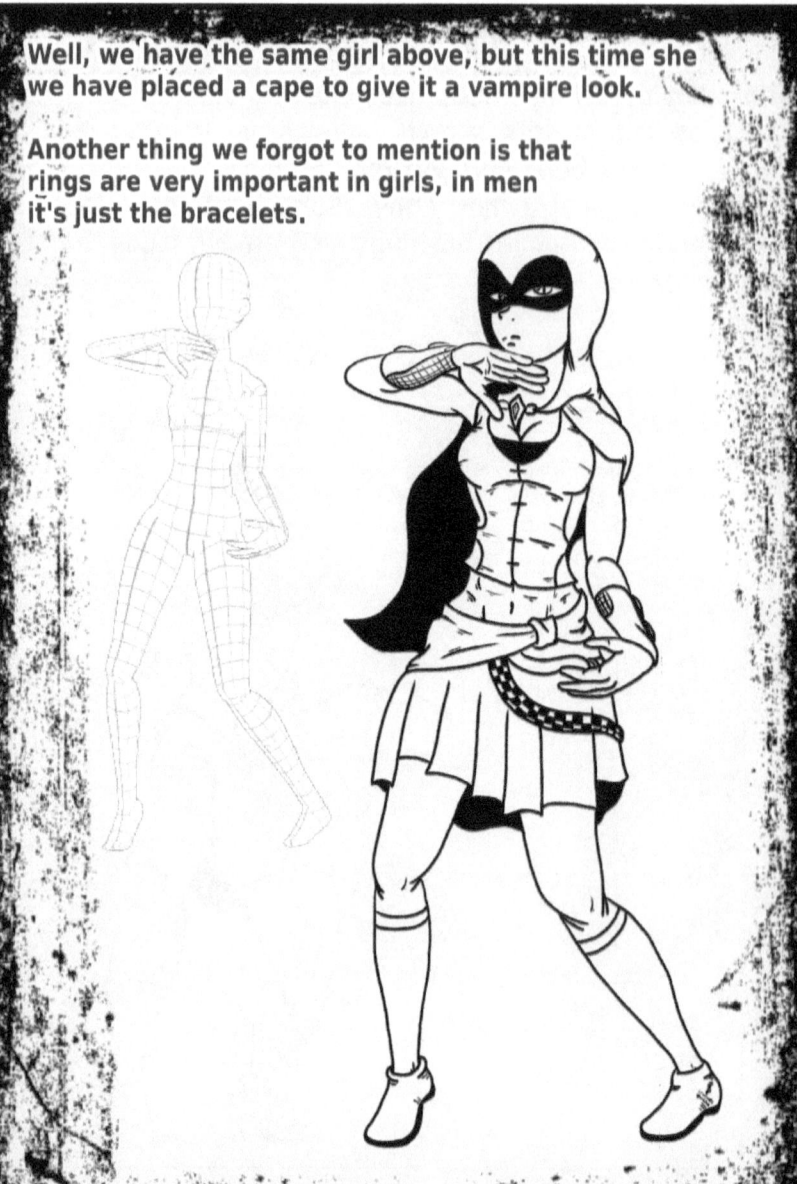

Finally we have the dark girl in positions that
they usually give an erotic or sick look.
The stockings are fishnet style (B), and the hollans again
they will never go out of use in this style (A).

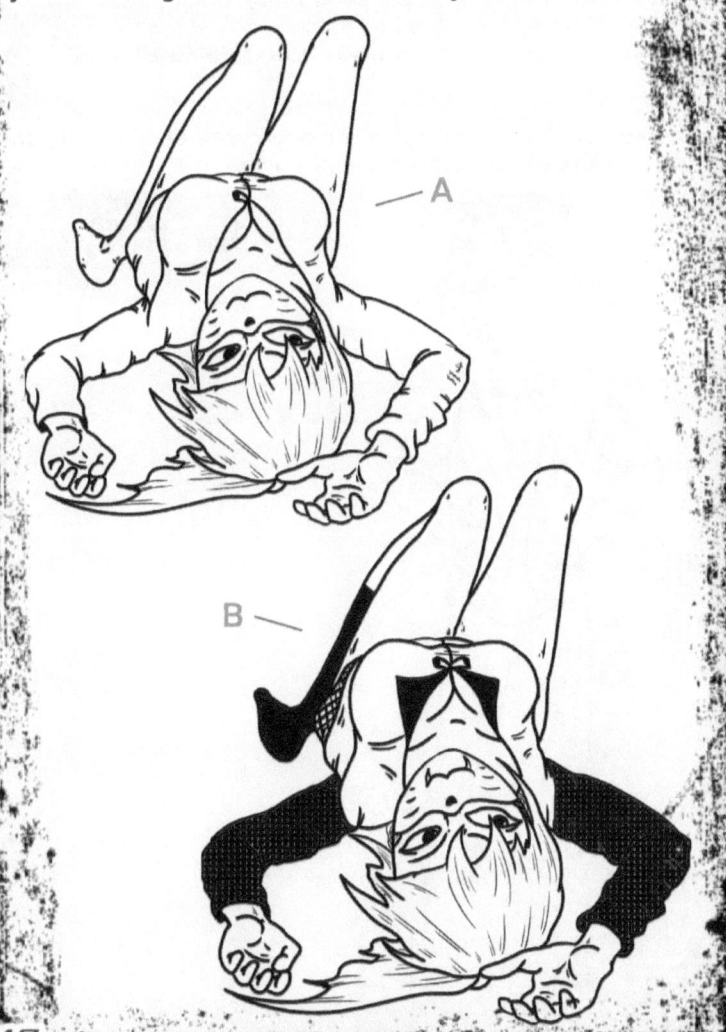

A

B

CLet's start now with the emos boys. This type of people wear very tight clothes, and very hairstyles rare. Many of you will say what an emo boy is. These they are called like that because of the emotions that one experiences, that's why the emos boys nickname. Anyway, the important thing in this manual is knowing how to draw hairstyles well, and personality.

The hair for these hairstyles must be very straight, as shown shown in the pictures above and on the left.

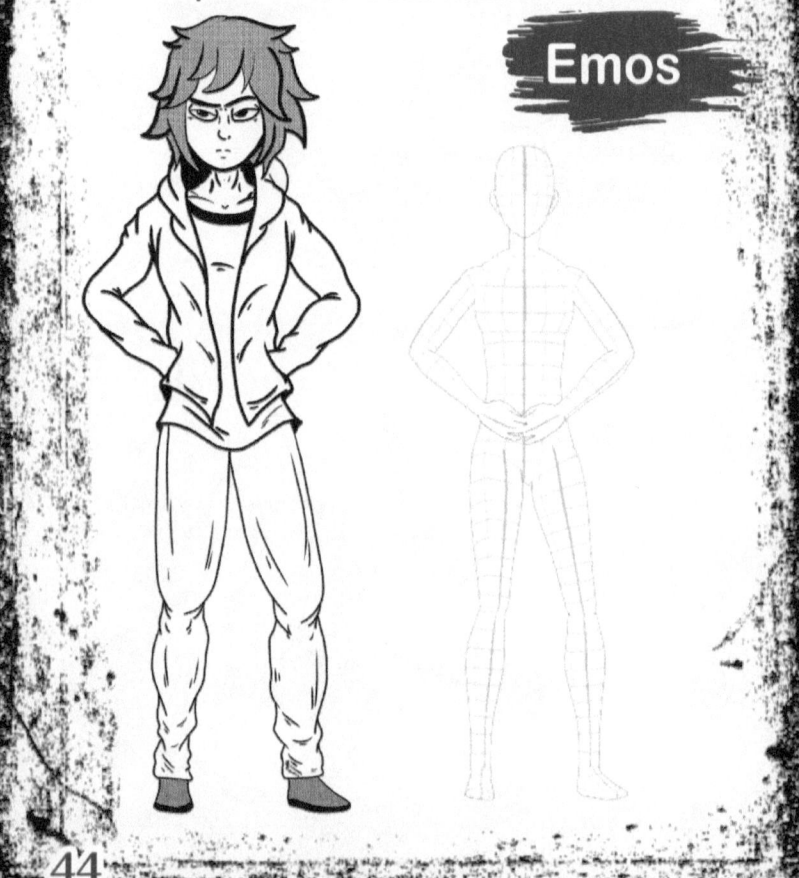

Emos

The hairstyle almost covers the entire face. Another option may be the broken hair, and cover the face with abundant hair of the character.

Here are some basic hairstyles. Good luck with your creations.

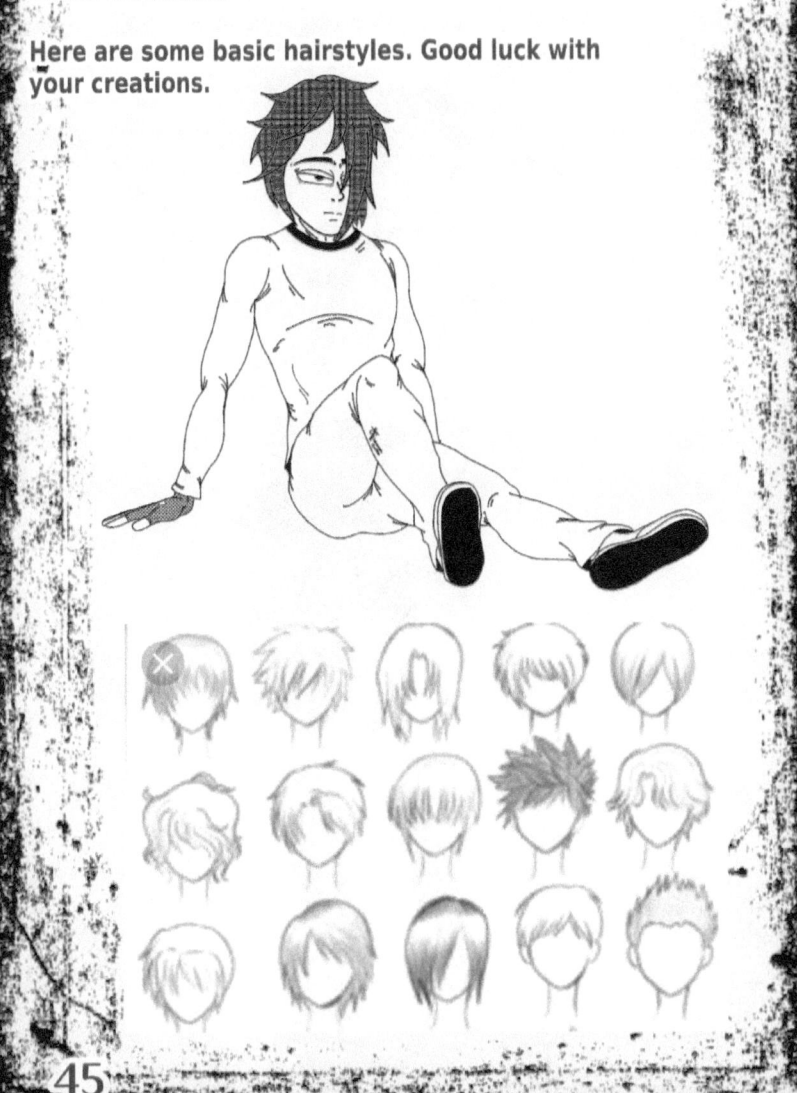

Emo clothes are very tight, as they usually
They are very thin and the features of the face are very
cadaverous. These boys' shirts are colored
red, black and blue, any but more red and black.
Many of them get to paint their eyes, and wear tennis type
slipper.

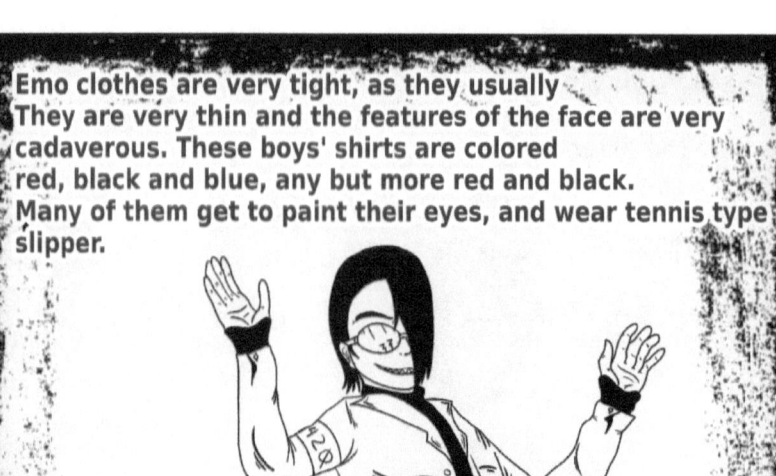

Here we have two examples of emo guys. Hairstyles
they cover the eyes and part of the nose. Like the darks,
many wear leather, canvas and fur bracelets. Others dress
black gloves with skull images.

The tennis shoes of the character on the left are checked,
but that does not mean that he is a skato, no, nothing
On the contrary, these sneakers mean that they support
the union between the black and white races, the same support
the skatos give it.

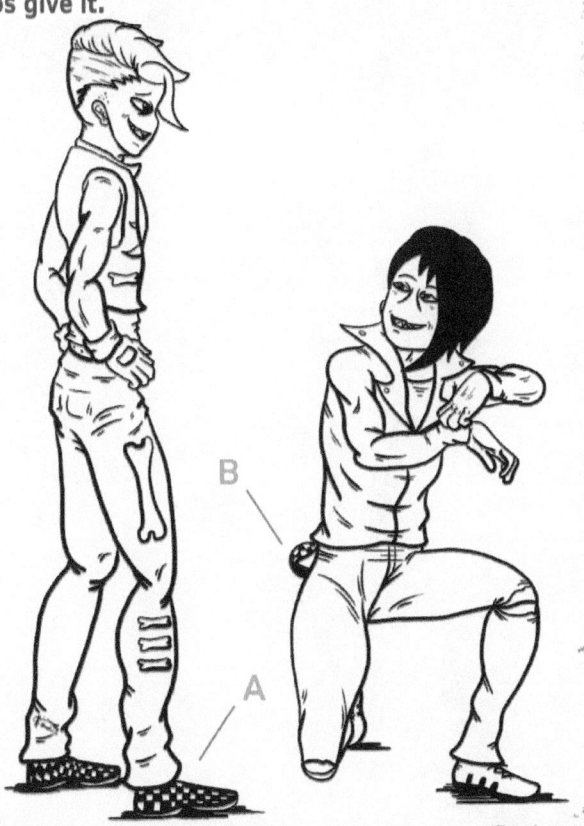

The punks are like the mix between emos, skatos and the darketos, but this only as an explanation, since the punketos exist long before all those mentioned.

These types of people are very aggressive in appearance and attitude, since just by looking at them you could say that they are vandals and that they would not behave well in any side.

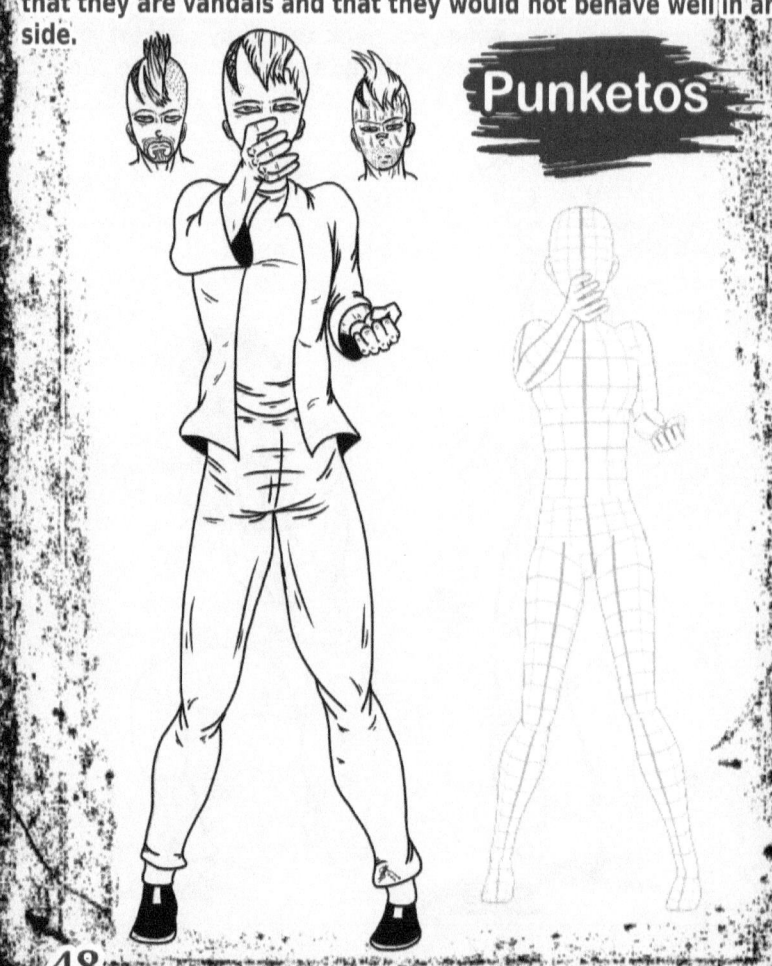

Punketos

To be able to draw this type of youth is very simple. He
hair is very sparse on the sides of the head and in abundance
in the middle.

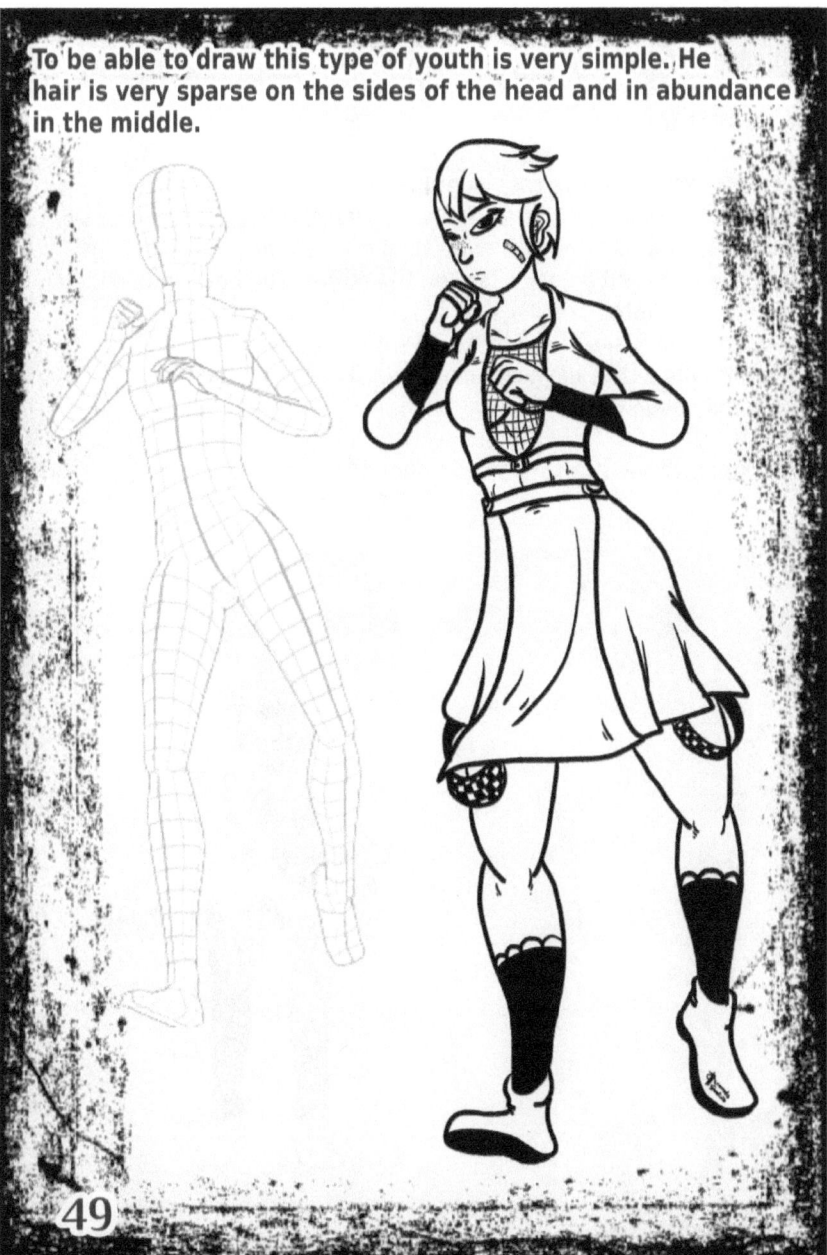

To end the punks, we can only say that the
three example youths are wearing blue jeans
army type (A).

Leather jackets, with peaks and tips to
give rudeness to our character, the big leather boots,
bracelets and hairstyle are more than enough for
this boy gave you a good scare on the street. The boy in the middle
His hair is painted and his shirt is torn. This serves to give you
more rudeness and wickedness. The bracelets are very different from
the left, since they have circular studs. The boots are
soft, but rough (B).

And the last one is a very simple punk (C).

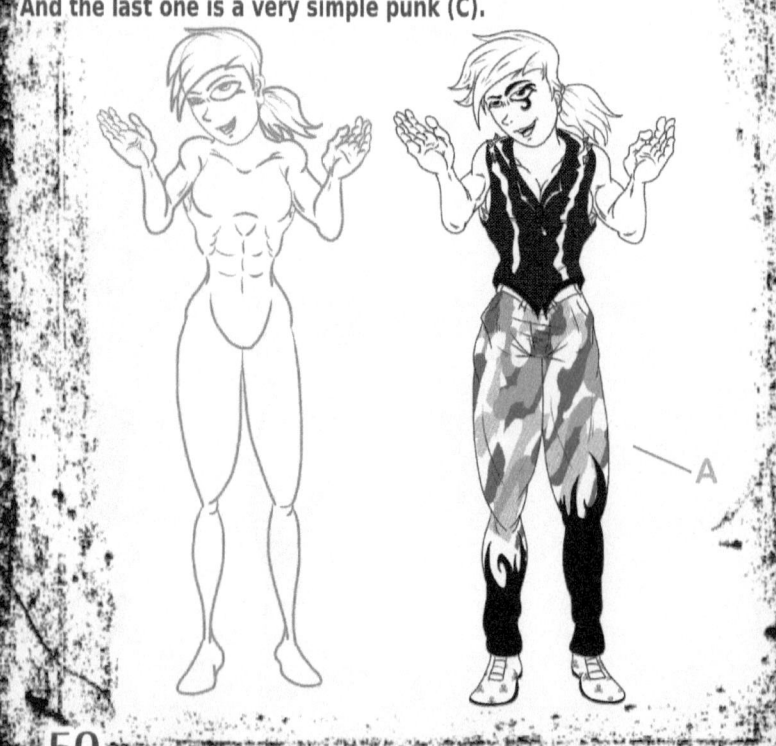

A

Well, considering who's who in your style of life and dressing, we can invent, combine clothes and clothe our character as we please. On this page you shows the base of a boy.

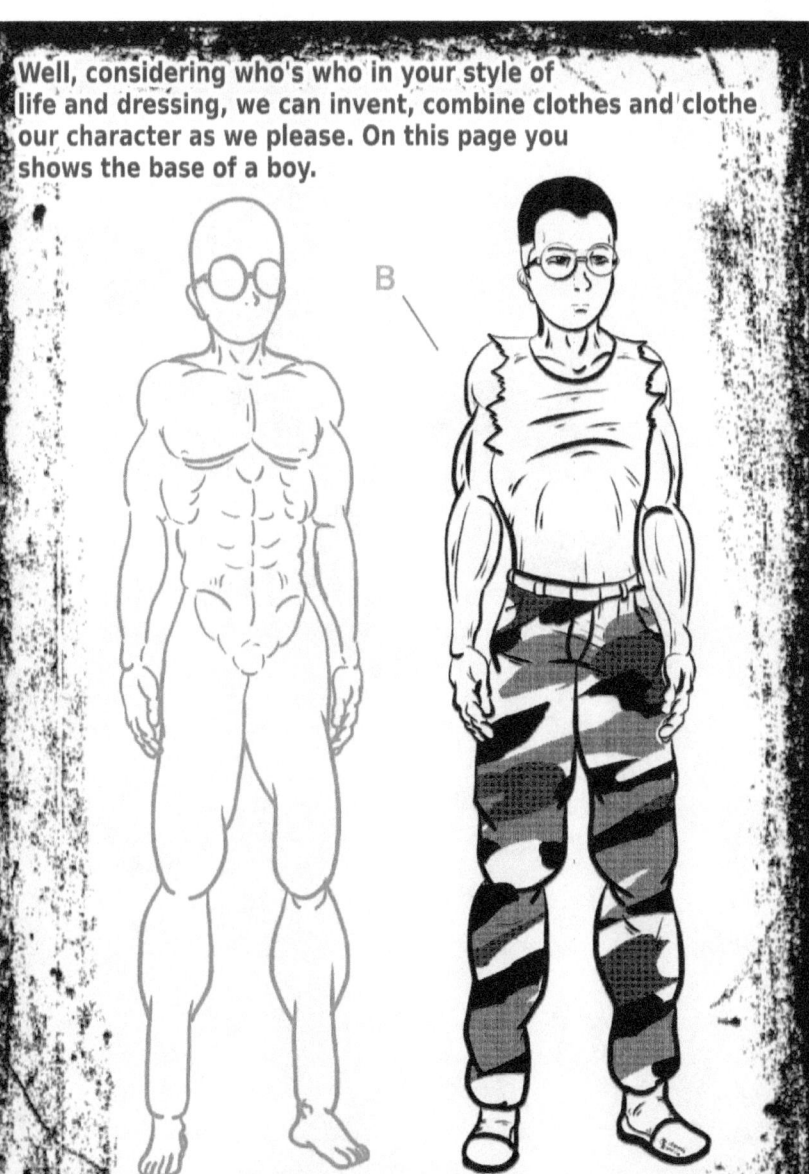

B

And finally,,we detail it so that later we can color it.
That was all. I hope it helps you a lot and you have learned
anything else.

See you soon.

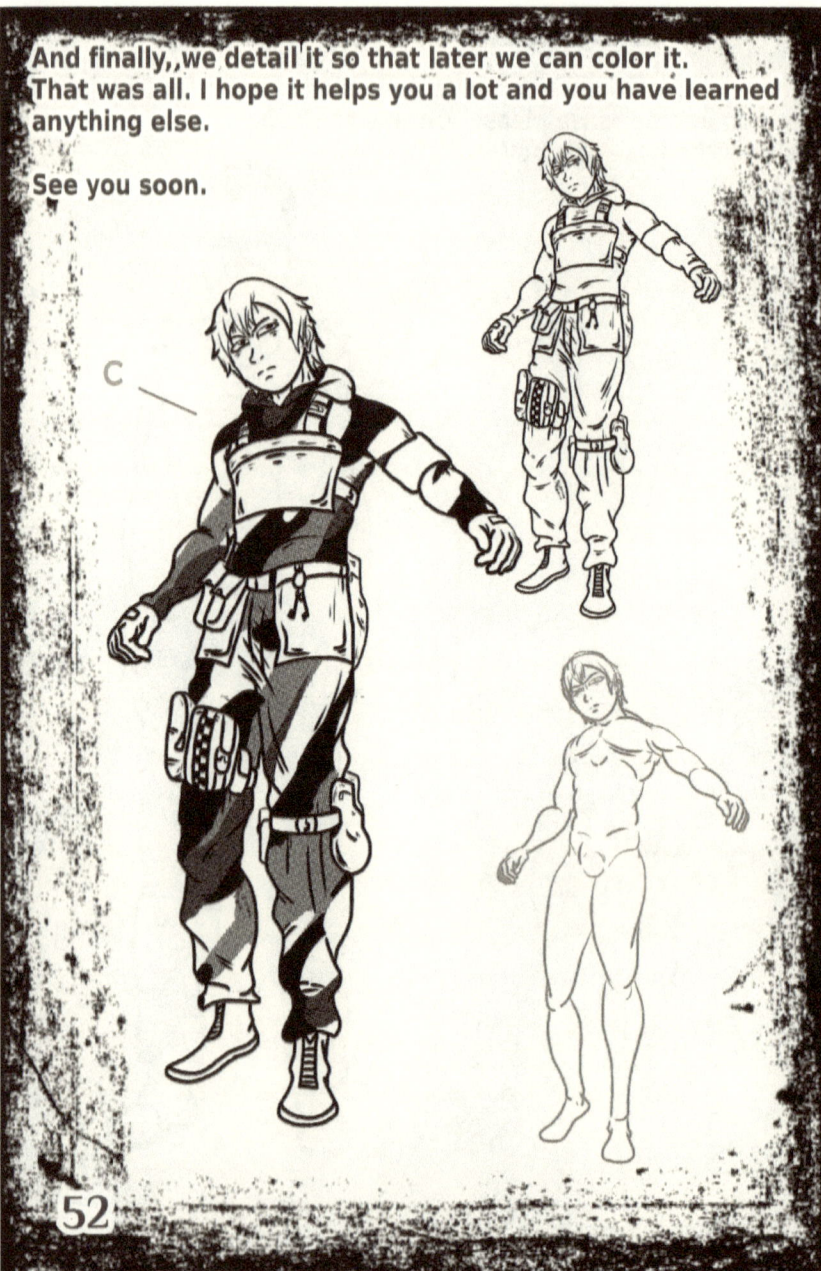

Characters of the book

(1) Lú Yán Lóng
(2) Lan Lóng
(3) Lao Zhang Long
(4) He Xian Lóng
(5) Han Xiang Long
(6) Zhongli Lóng
(7) Cao Jing Long
(8) Li Lóng
(9) Ip Tao Lóng (Huánglóng)
(10) Tao Meik Long

1. Ng Mui (Huánglóng couple)
2. Xi Mui (Mother of Ng Mui)
3. Yu Mui (Ng Mui's father)

1. Yang Lóng (Father of Huánglóng)
2. Yin Lóng (Mother of Huánglóng)

1. Uma Meik (Daughter Táo Meik)
2. Sun Lóng (Disciple Huánglóng)
3. Lix Lóng (Daughter of Lú Yán)
4. Zum Lóng (Son of Lao)
5. Wu Sau Lóng (Son of Han Xiang)
6. Tang Lóng (Son of Lao)
7. Siu Lóng (Son of He Xian)
8. Lán Sho Lóng (Son of Cao Jing)
9. Jet Lóng (Daughter of Lú Yán)
10. Kiu Lóng (Daughter of Lan)
11. Gao Lóng (Daughter of Li)
12. Chén Sho Lóng (Son of Zhongli)
13. Chang Lóng (Han Xiang's daughter)
14. Wang Lóng (Son of Xian Lóng)

1. Kuramochi Jamsan (Mr. Pulpomo)
2. Ariel Lóng (Dicipulo Huánglóng)
3. Jhoanna (Kuramochi's partner)
4. Sari (Daughter of Kuramochi)
5. John (Son of Kuramochi)
6. Chrono Visor (character)
7. Chrono Viewer (Artifact)
8. Gonk Lóng (Son of Sun)

1. Mao Spartan (Chip's twin sister)
2. Chip Spartan (Huánglóng's brother in arms)
3. Ling Spartan (Mao's Sister)
4. Adrammelech Lóng (Huánglóng's adoptive older brother)
5. Qing Lóng (Dicipulo Huánglóng)
6. Rin Lóng (Huánglóng couple)

Additional Special Comic in the purchase of the Manual.

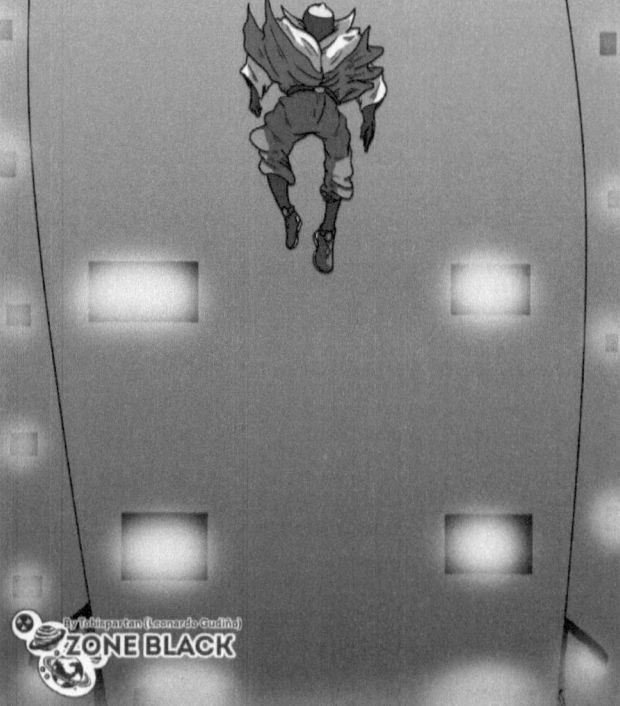

All Eye On Me

By Tubispartan (Leonardo Gudiña)
ZONE BLACK

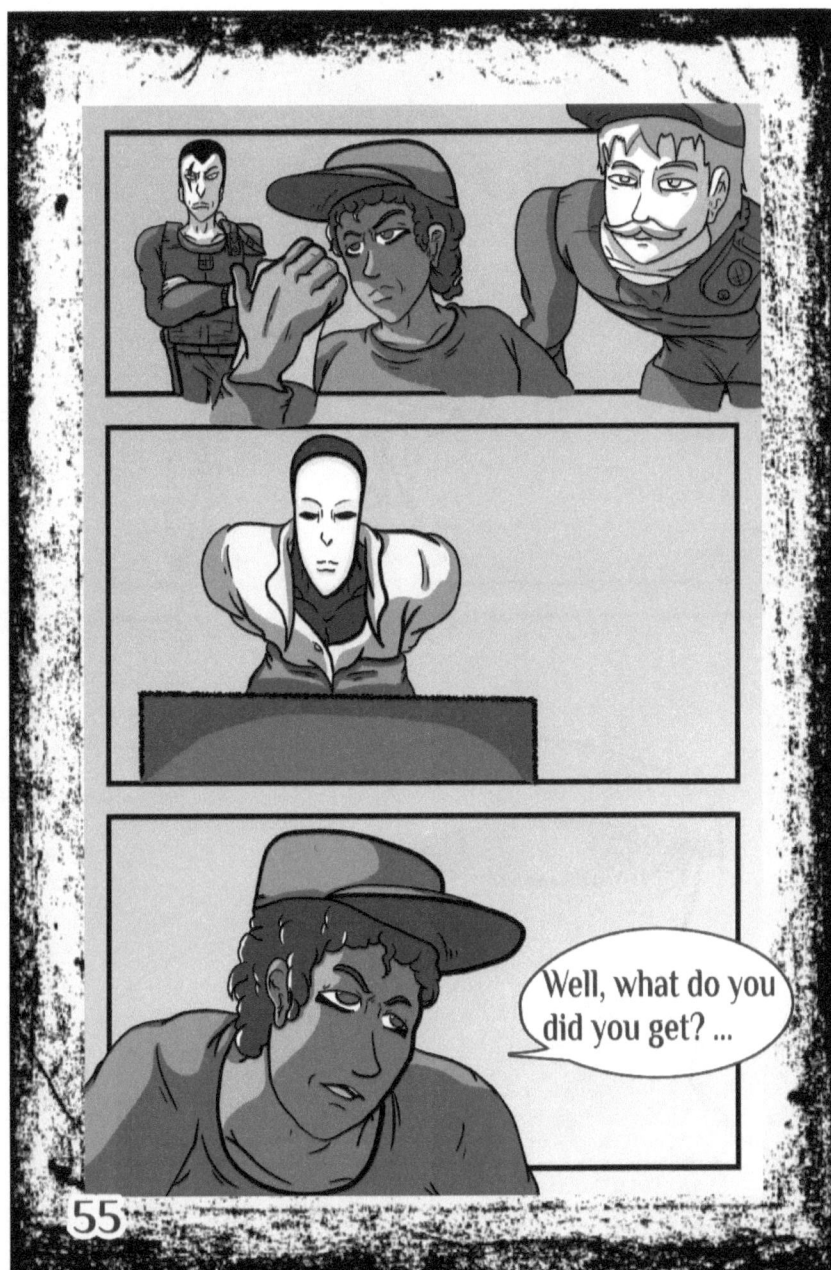

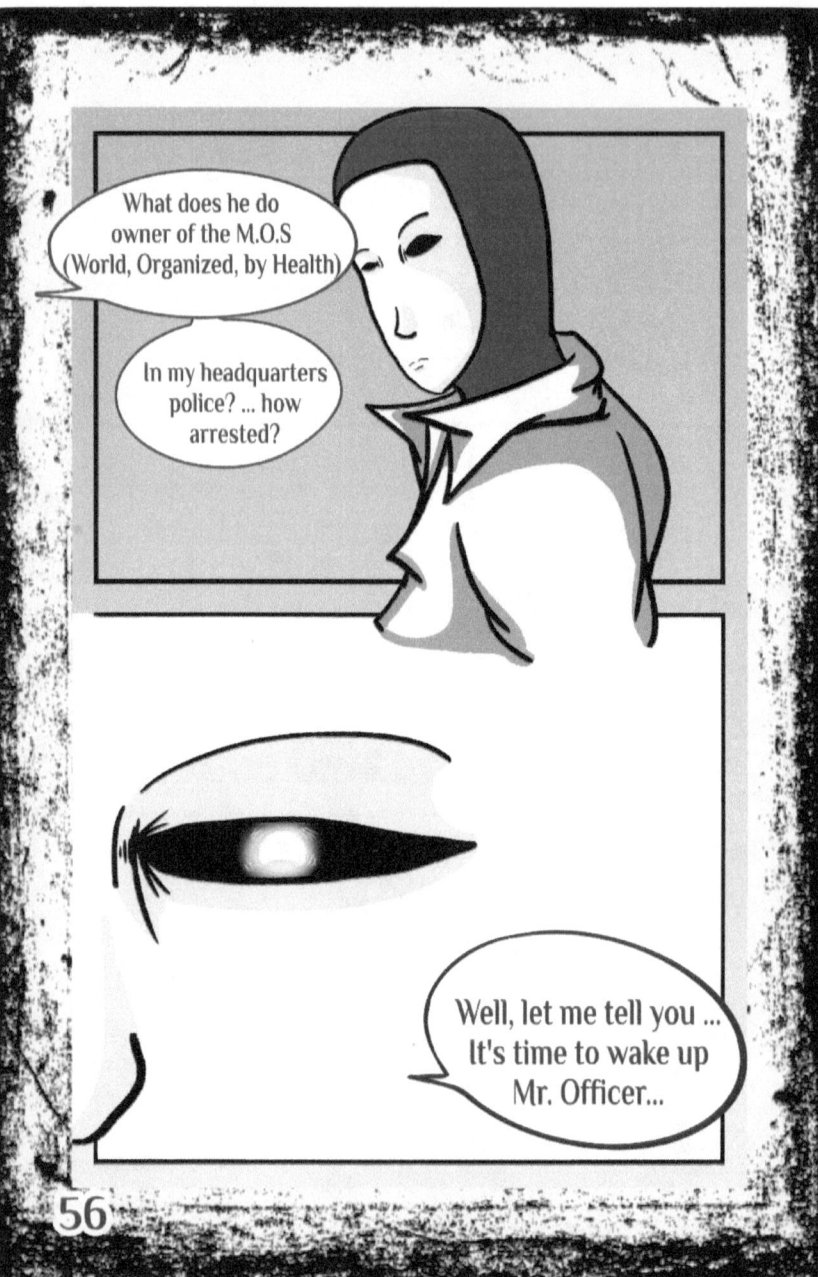

56

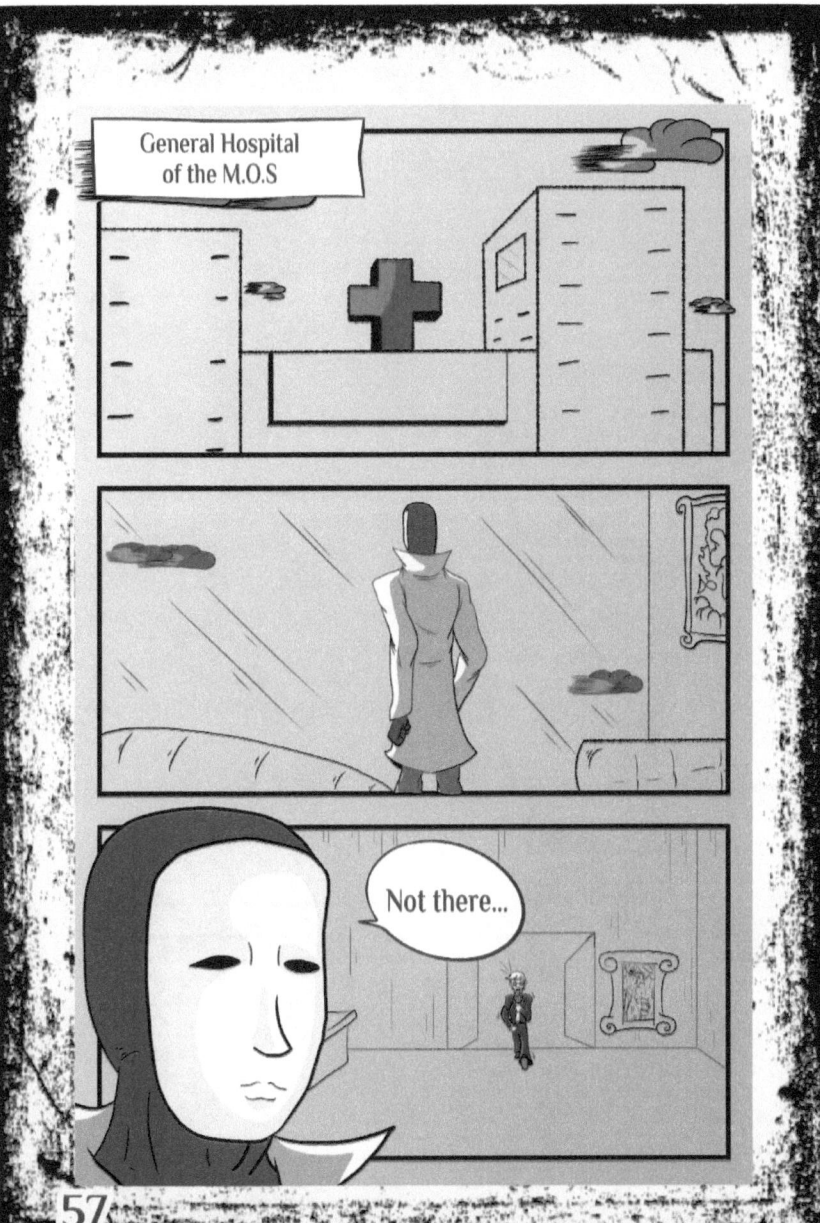

General Hospital of the M.O.S

Not there...

57

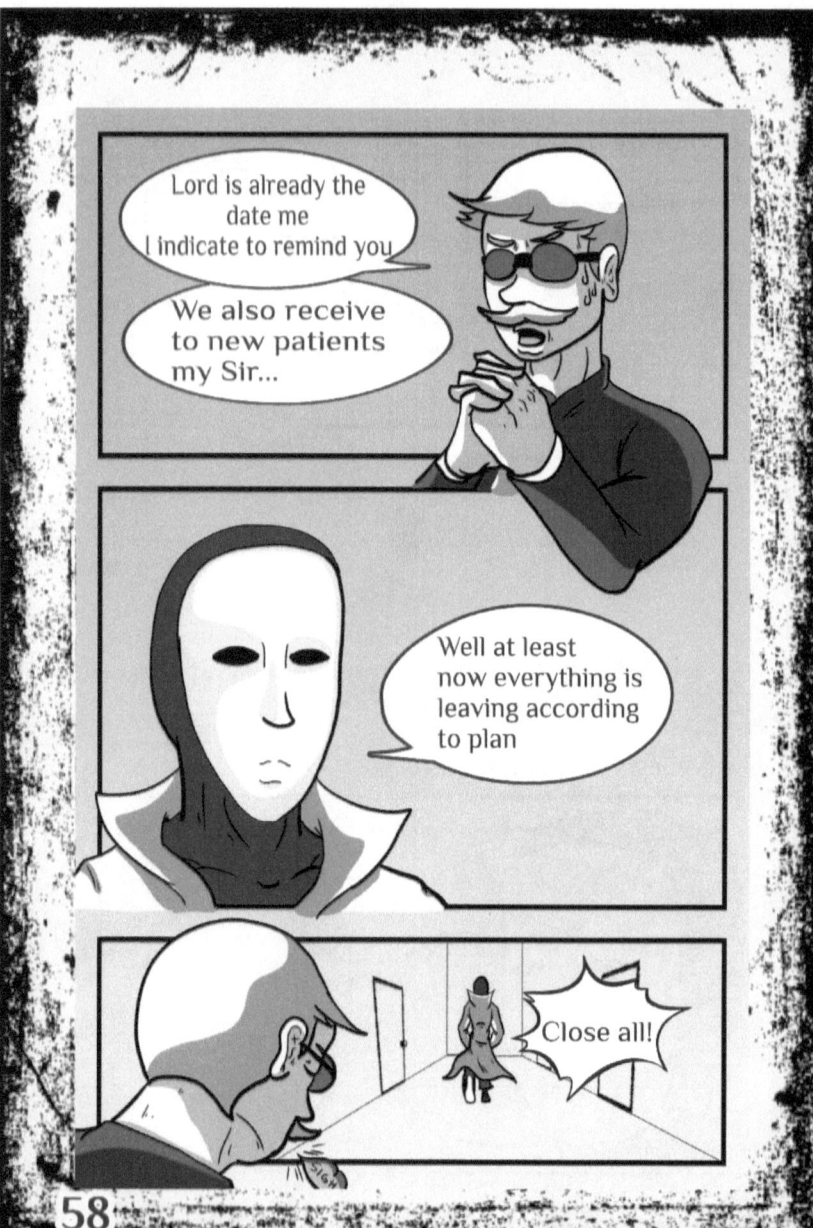

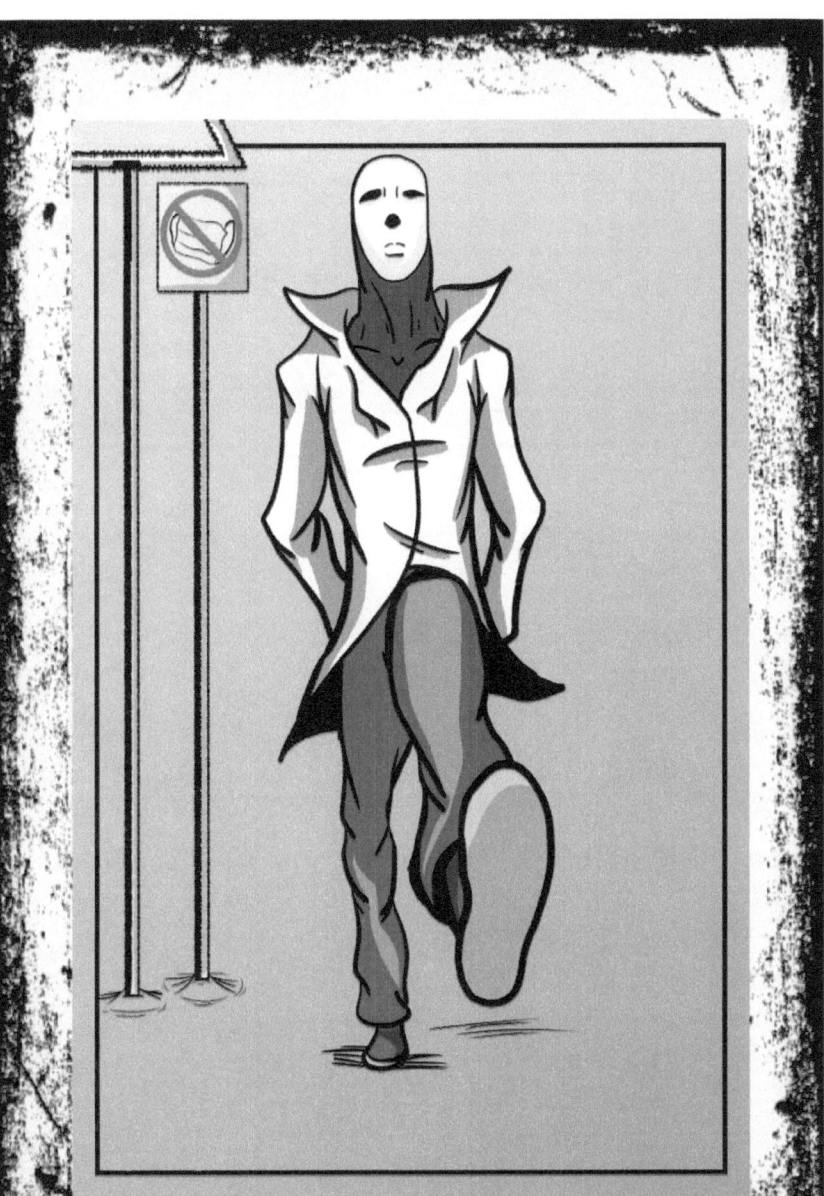

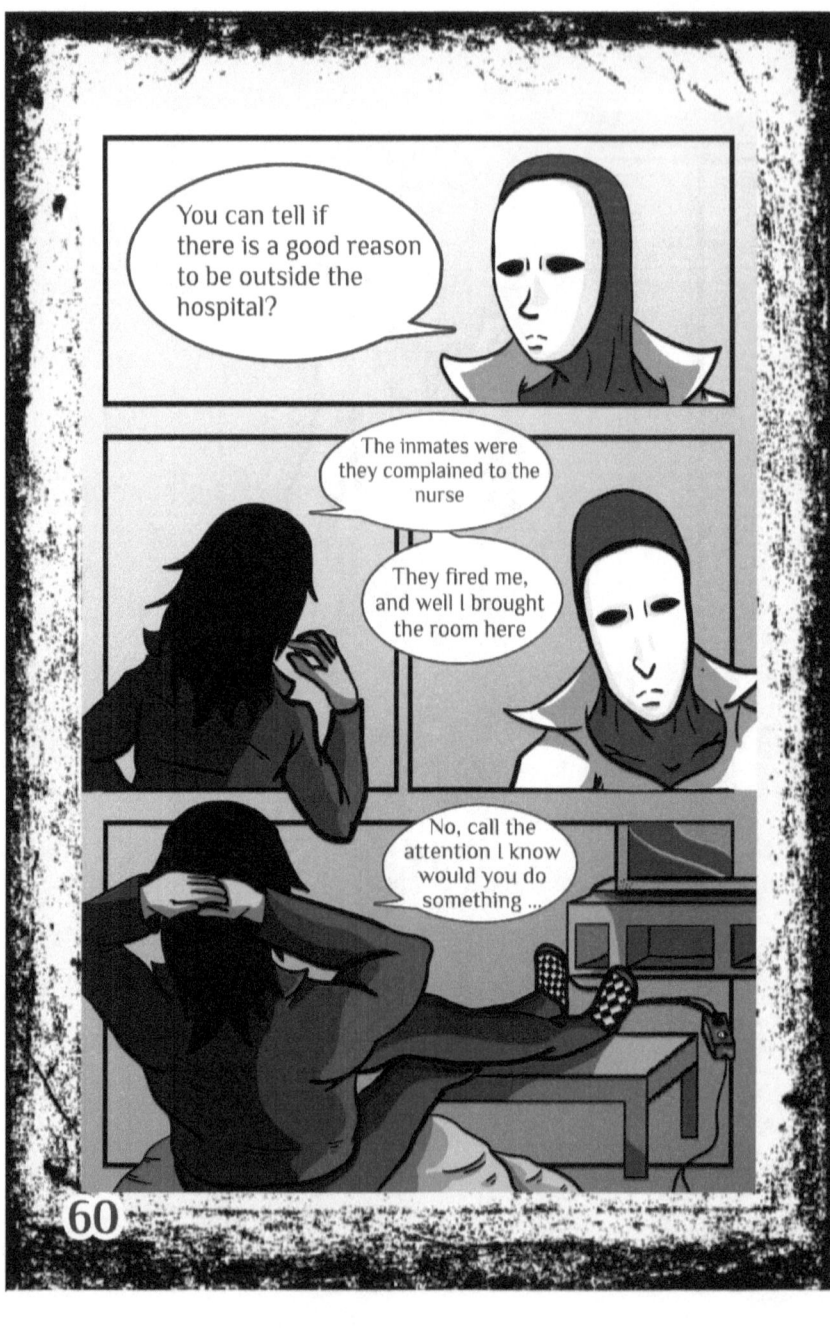

60

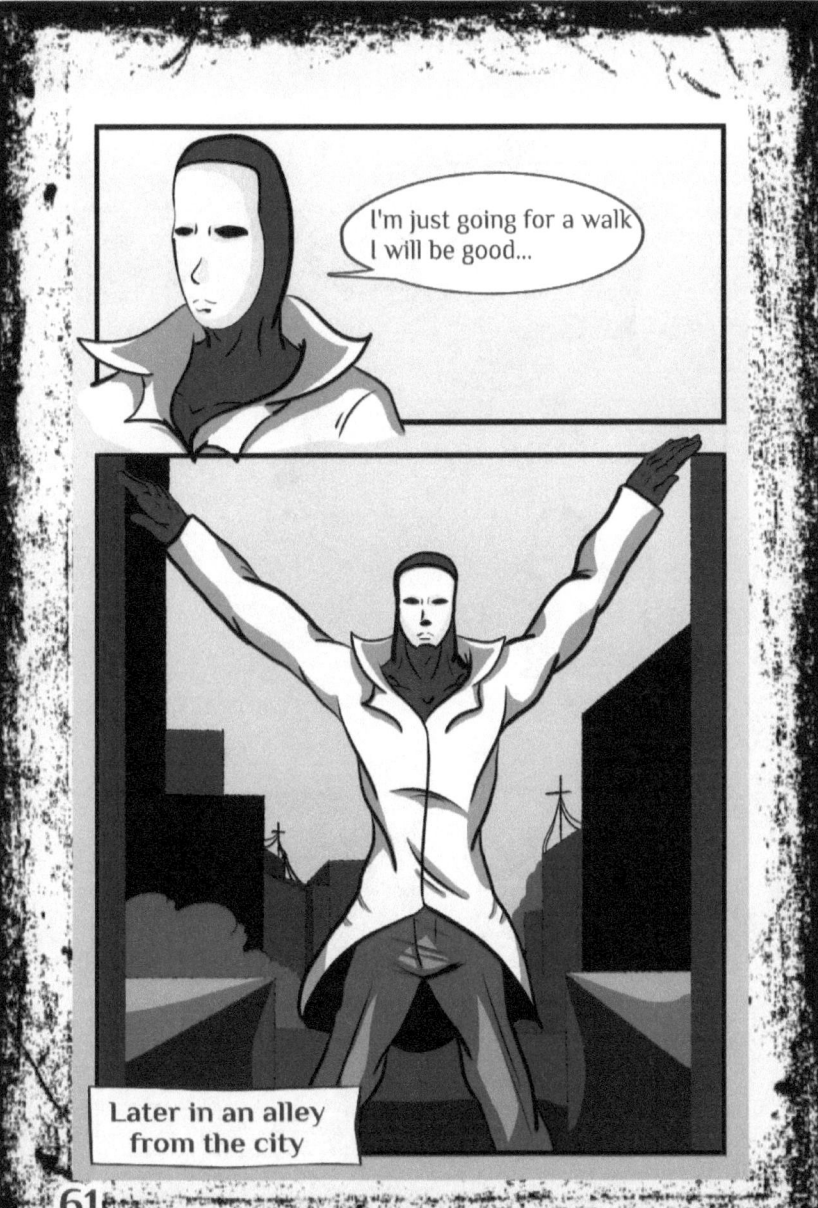

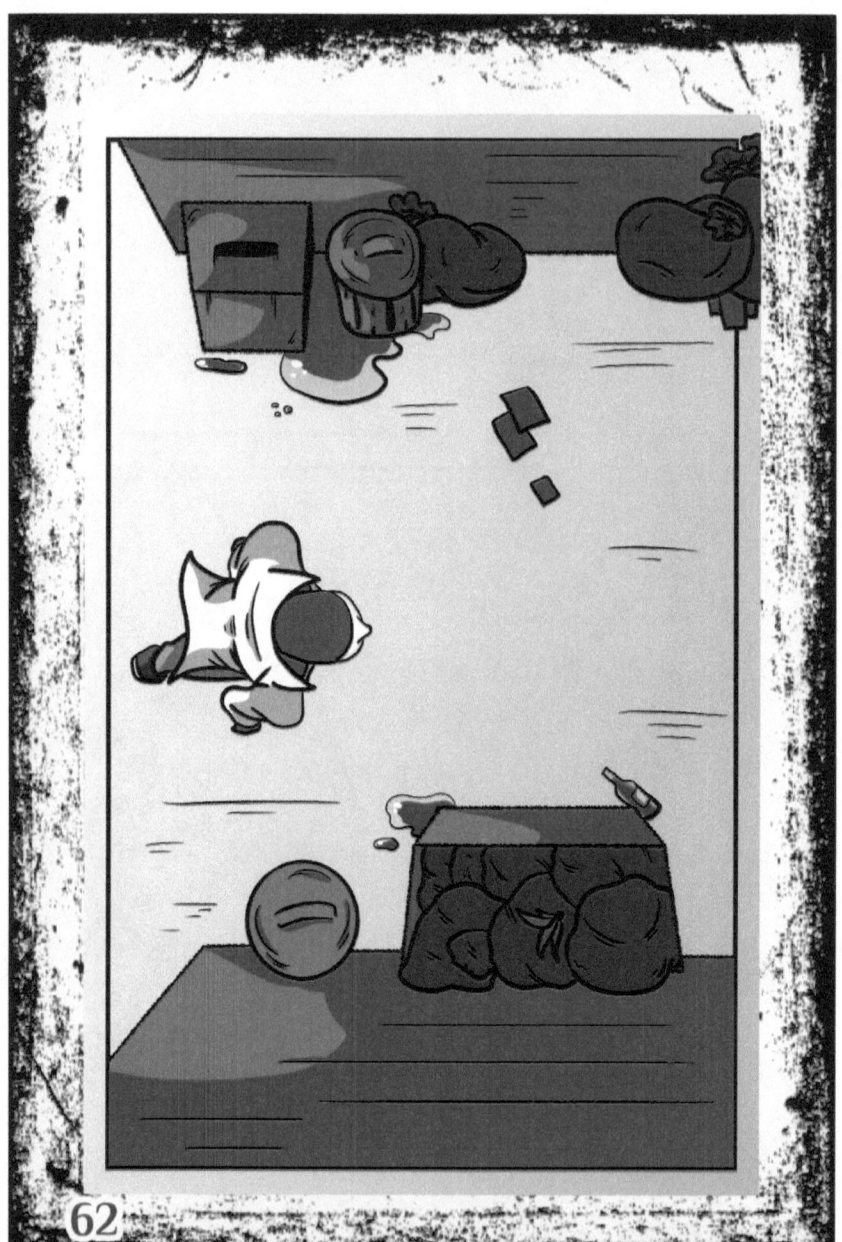

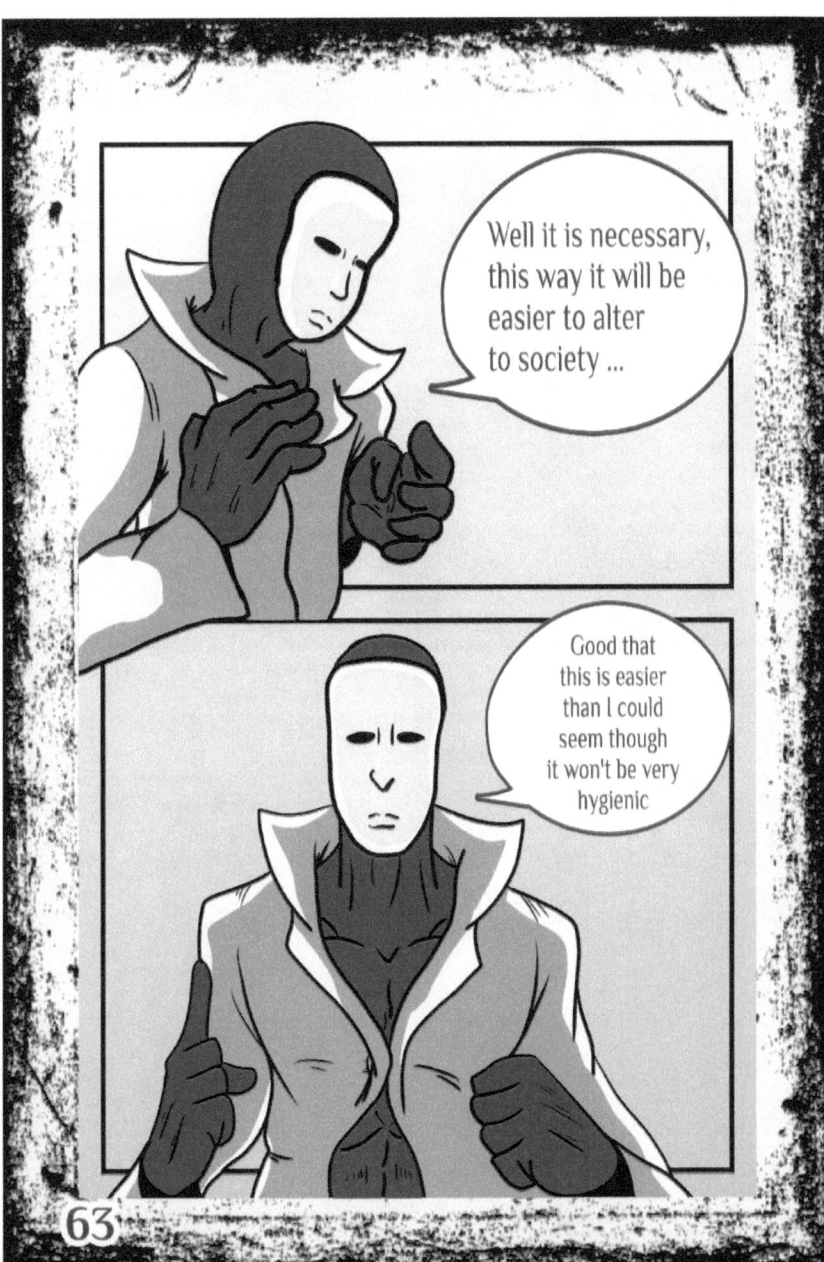

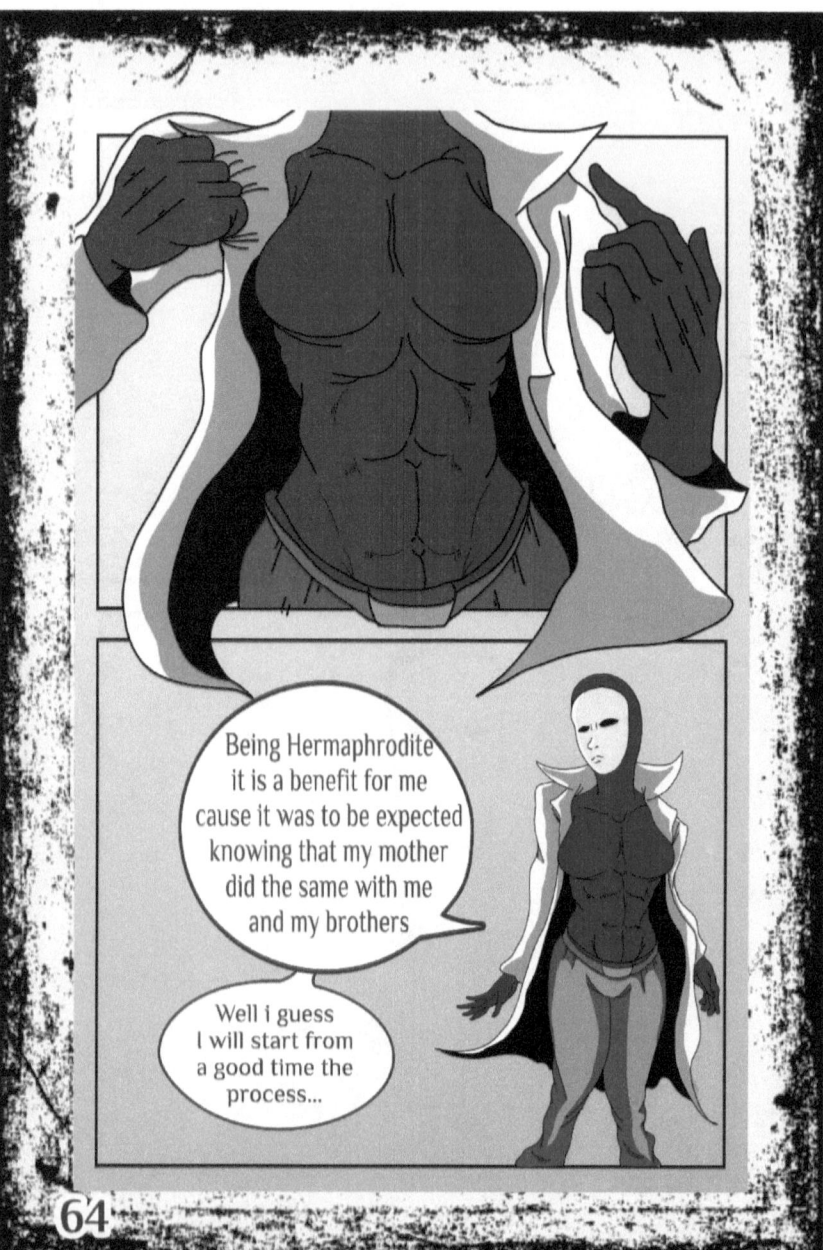

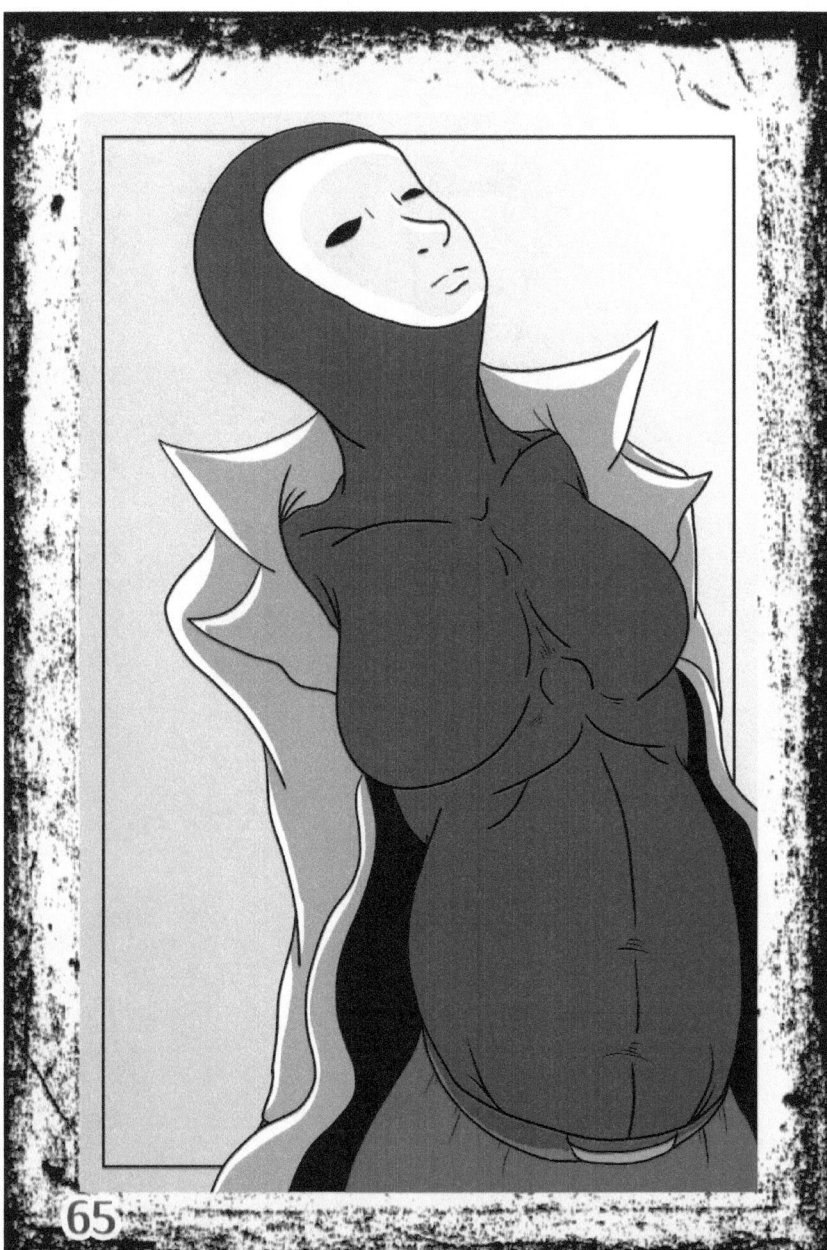

65

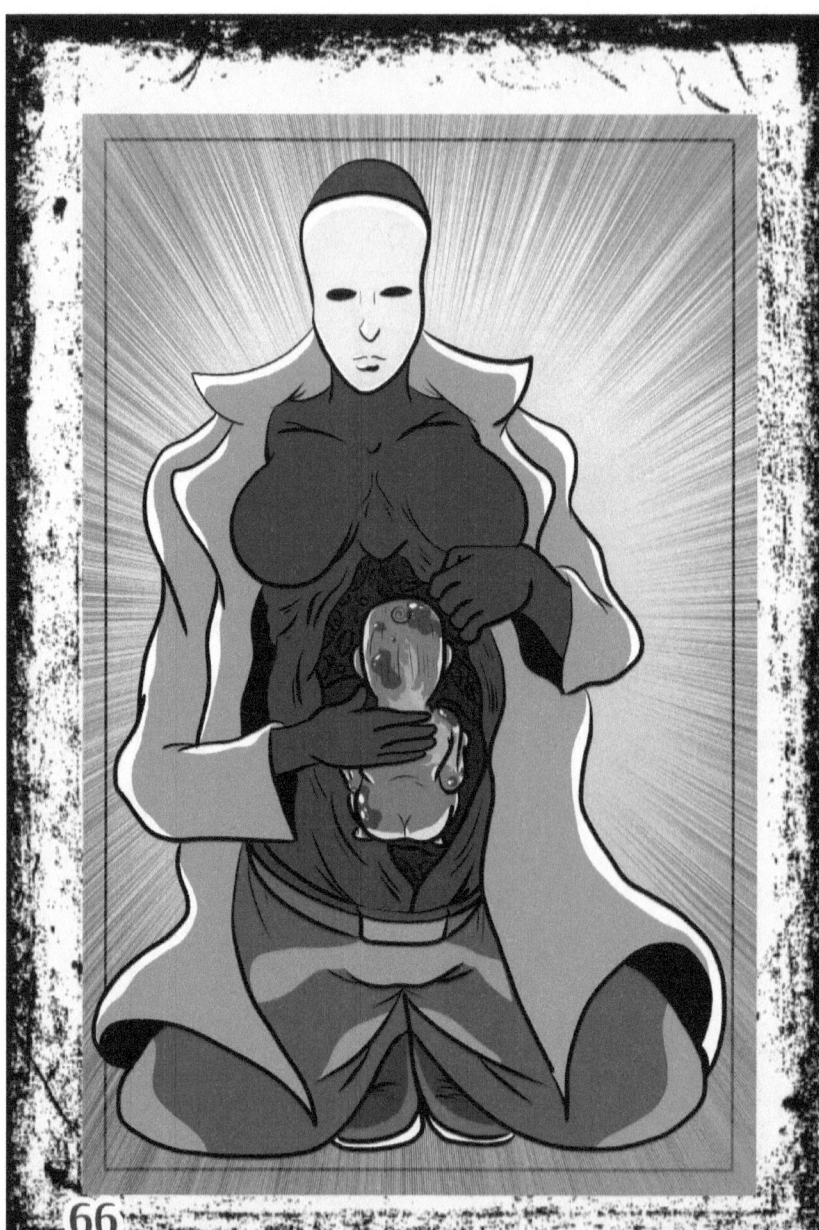

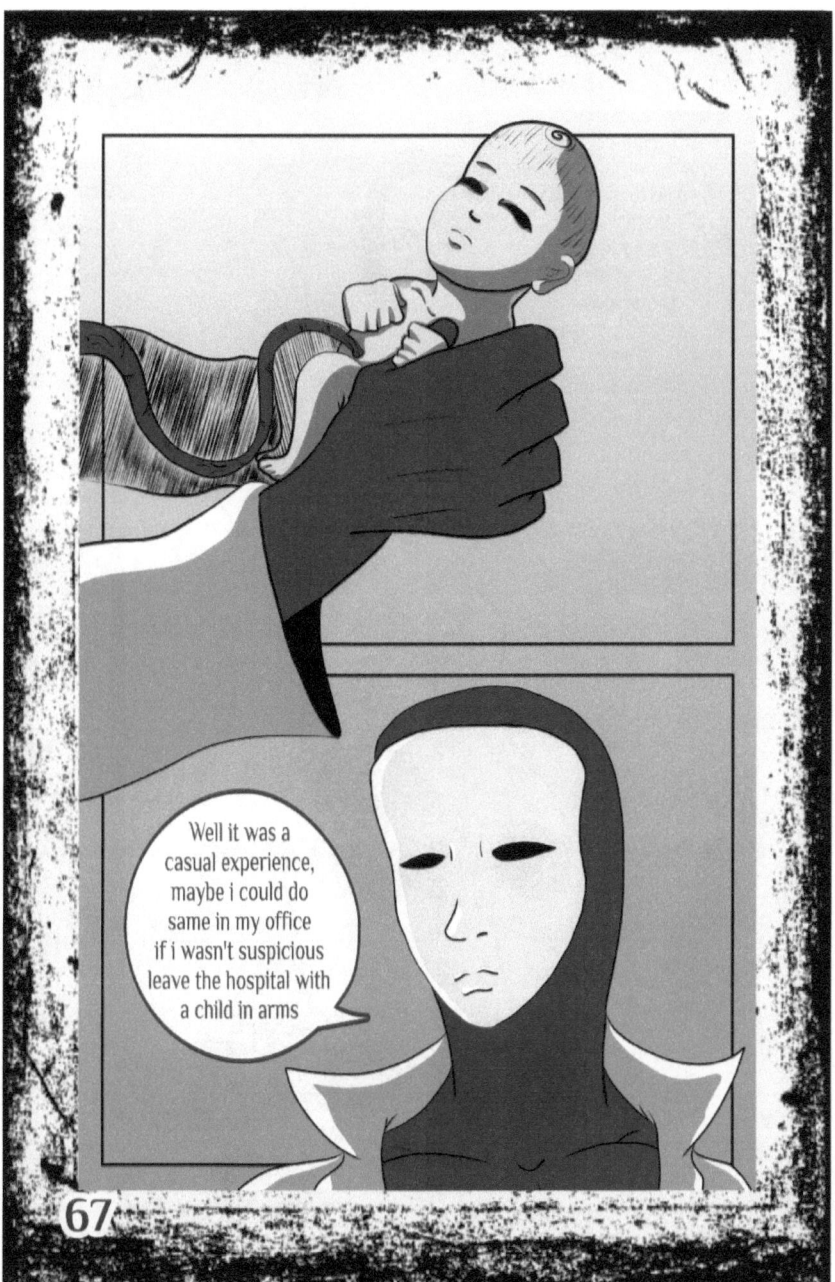

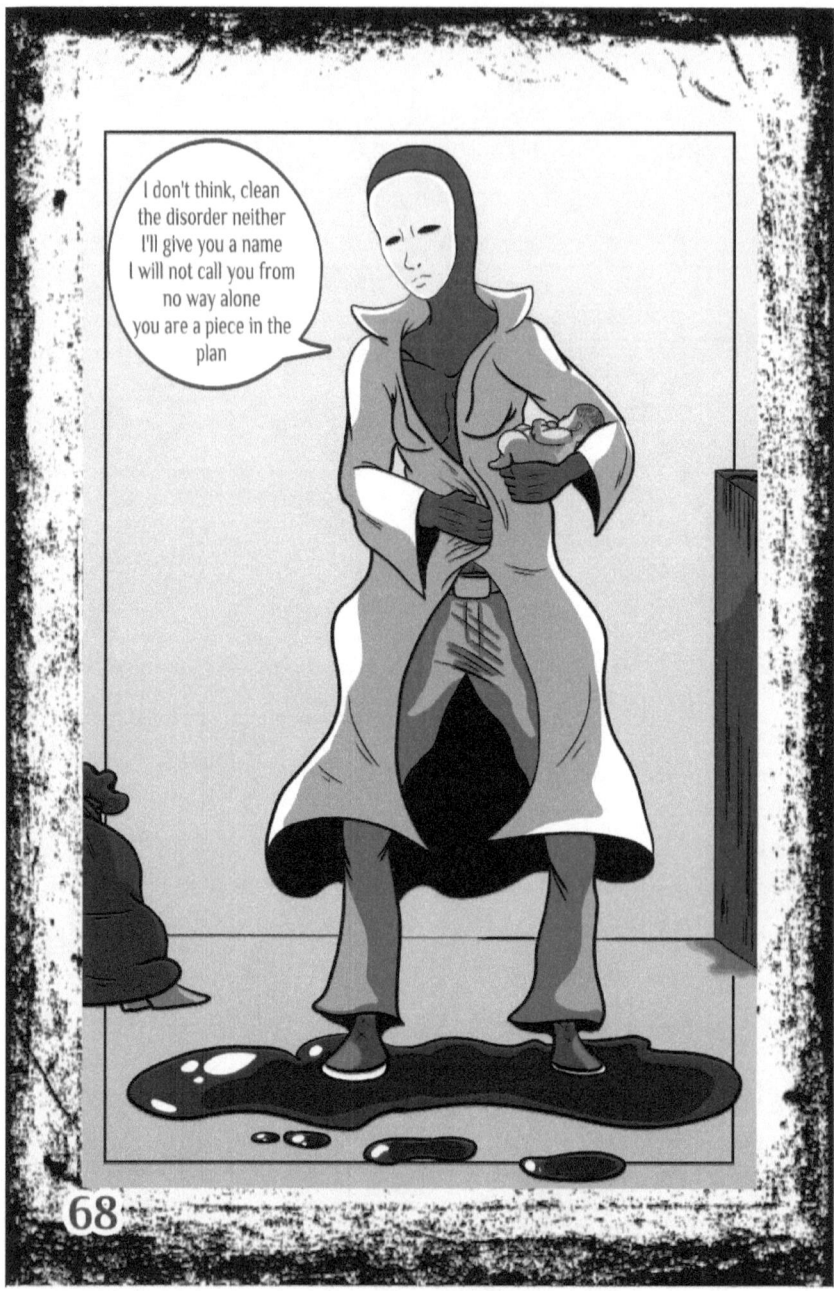

68

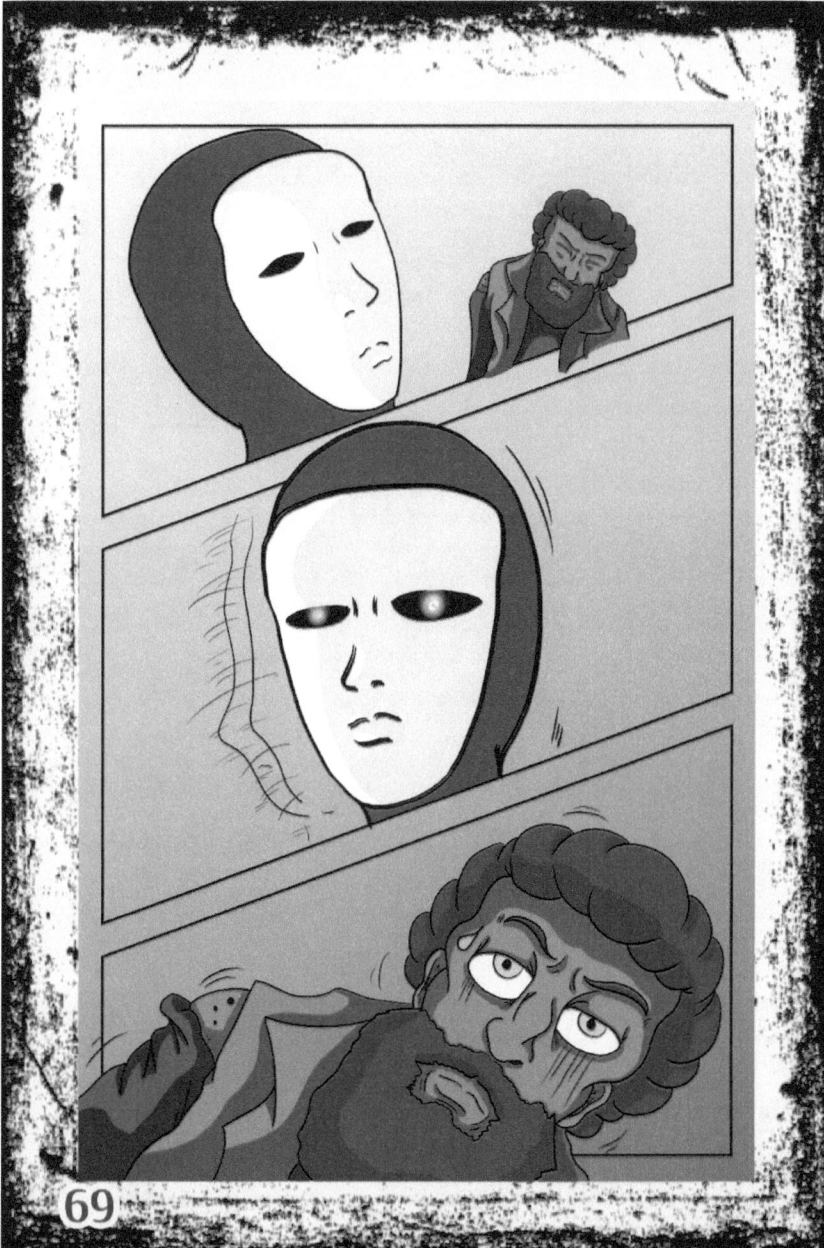

69

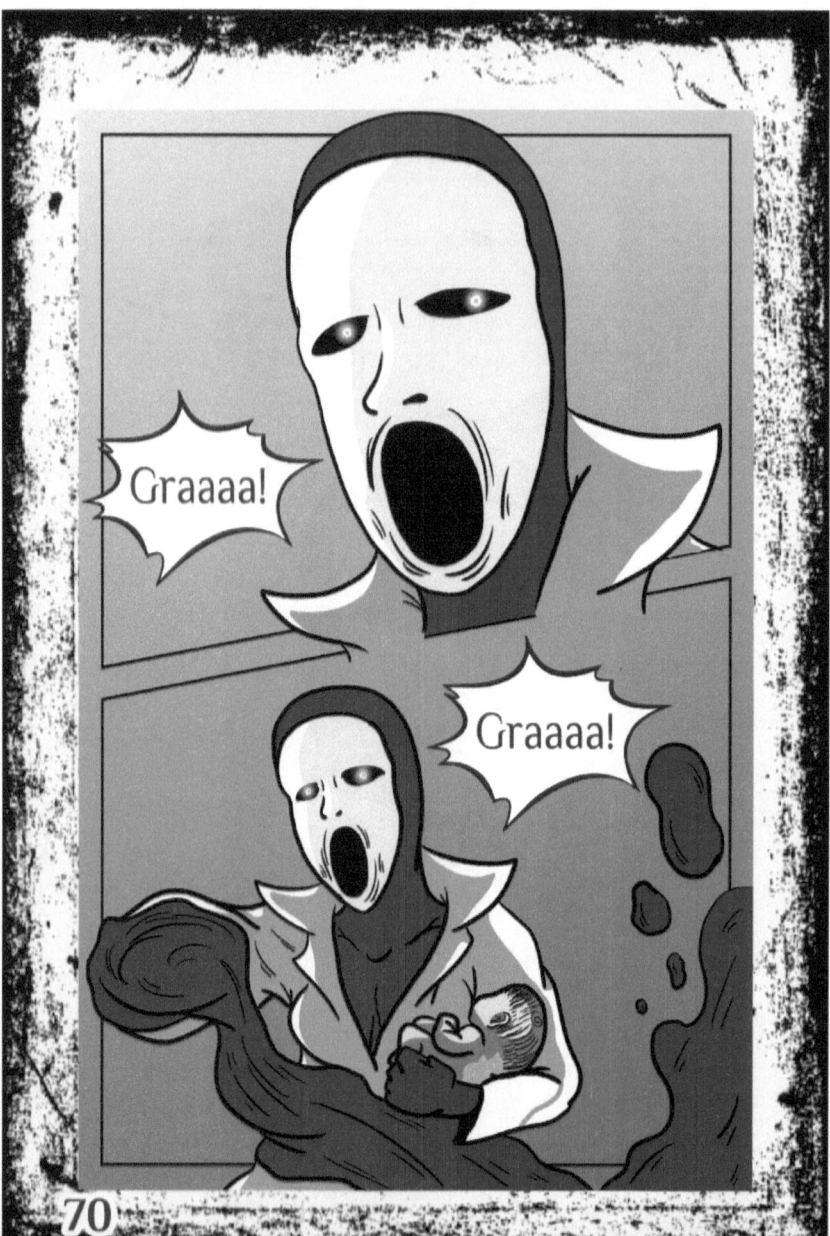

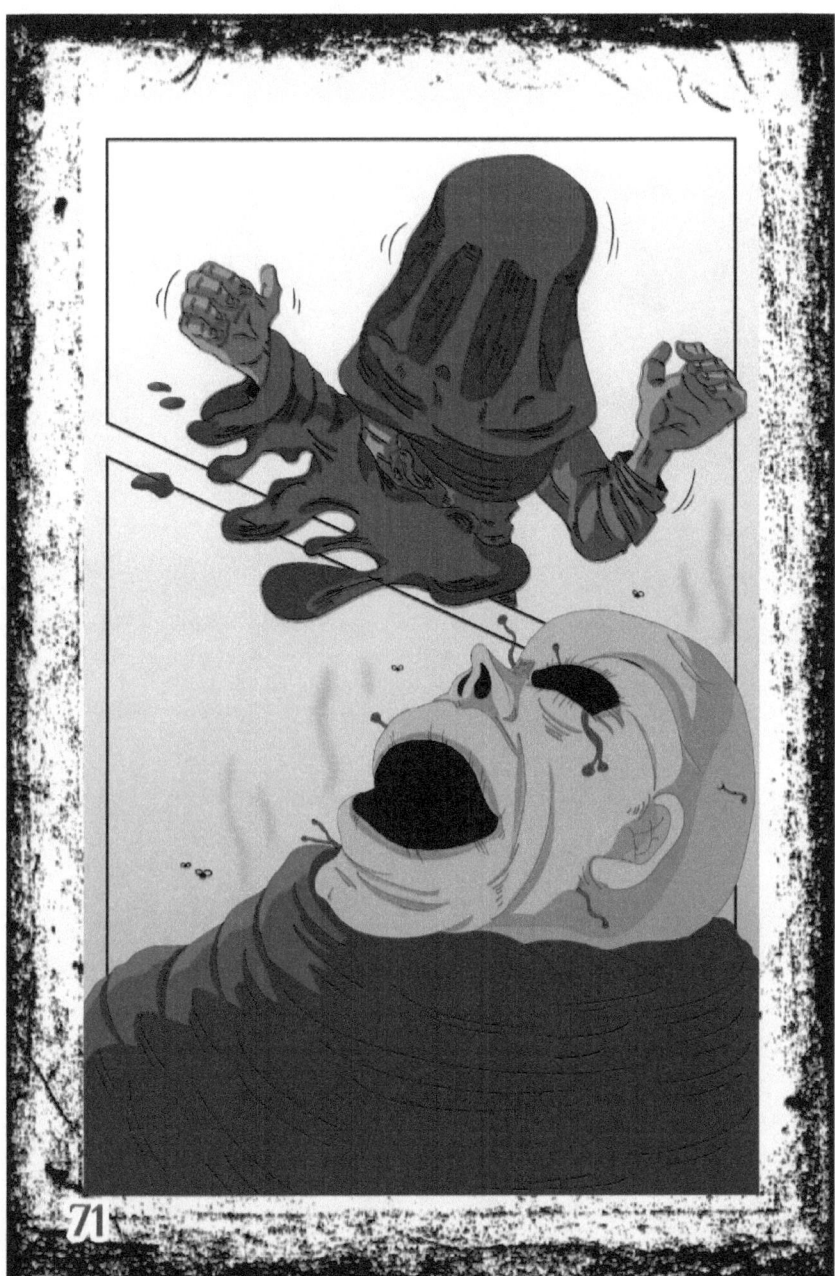

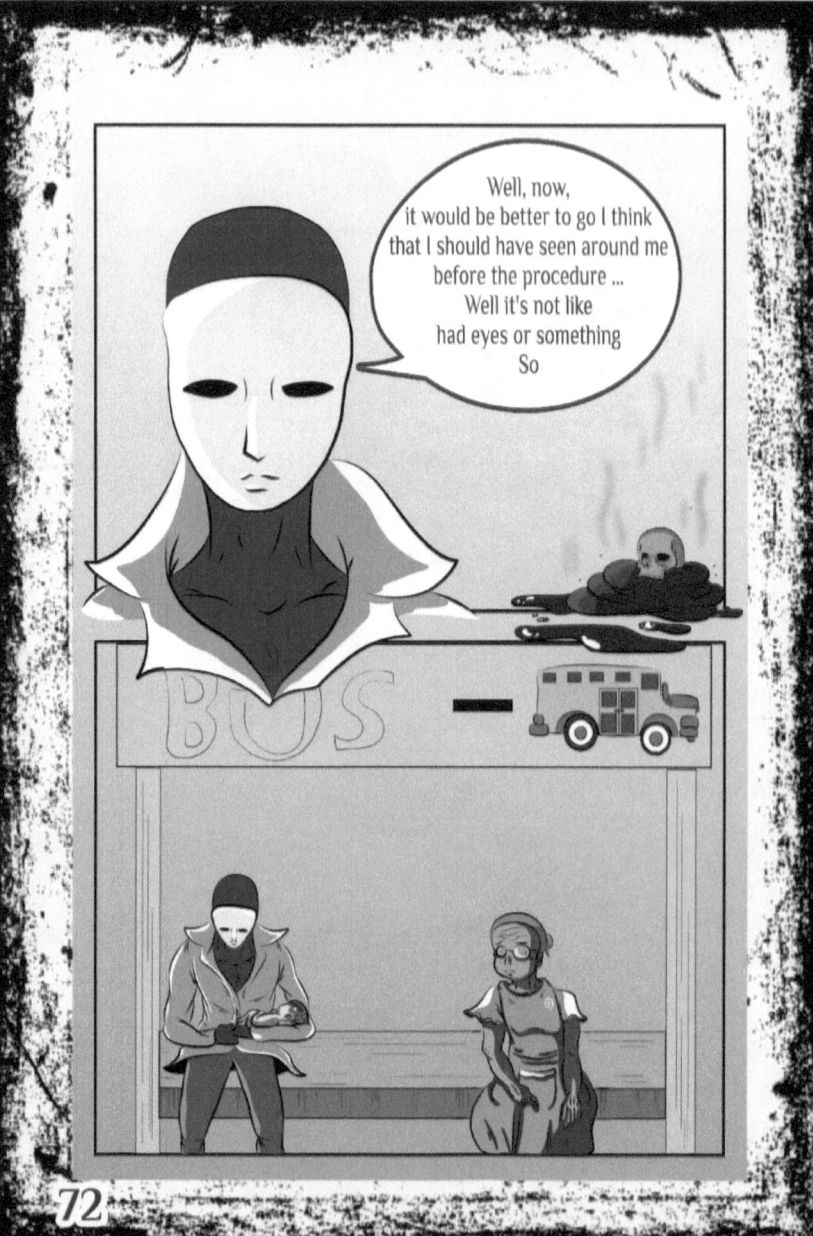

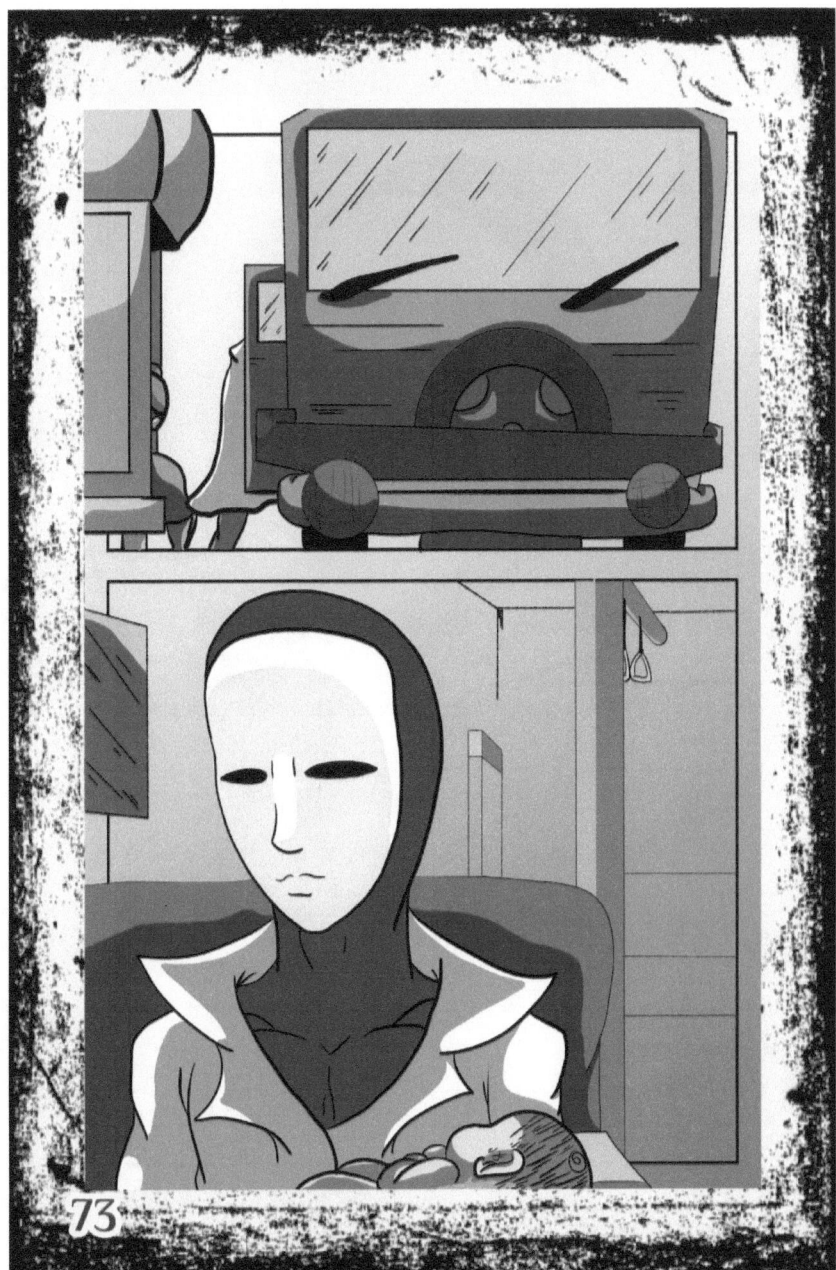

73

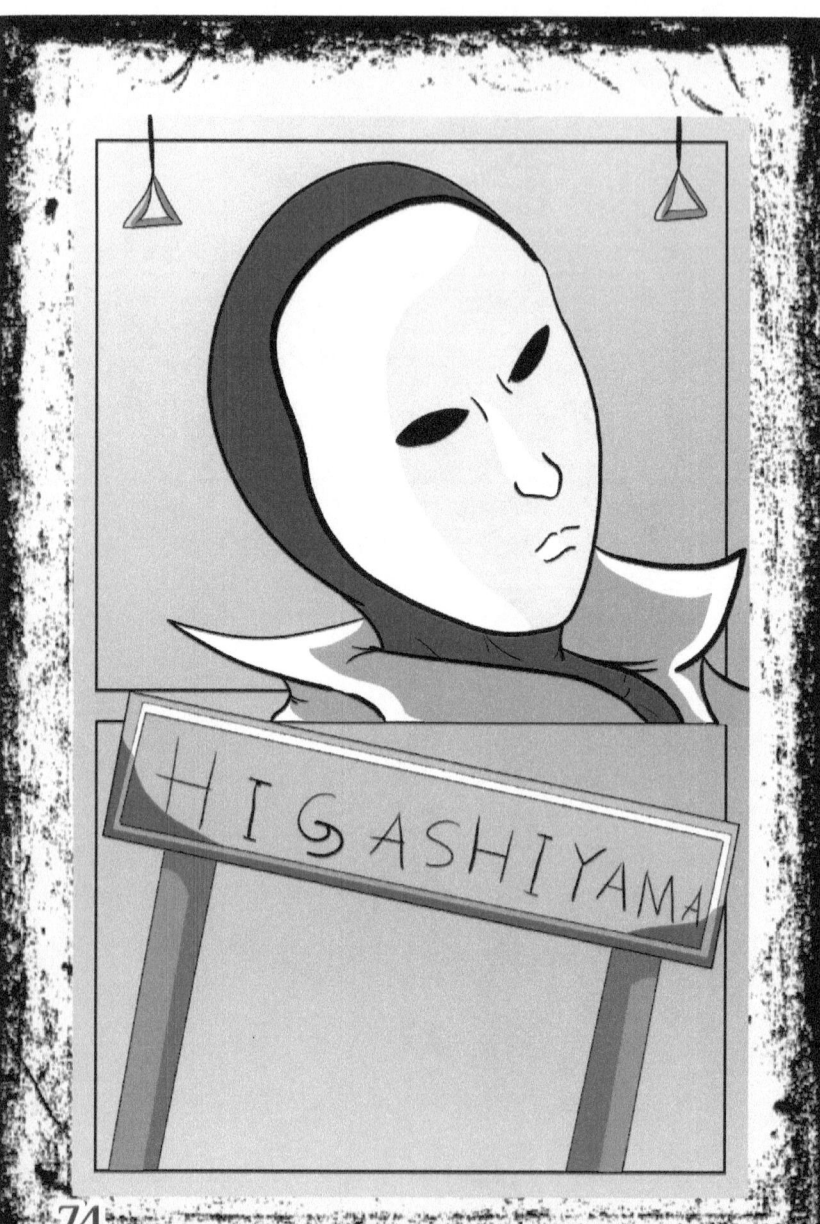

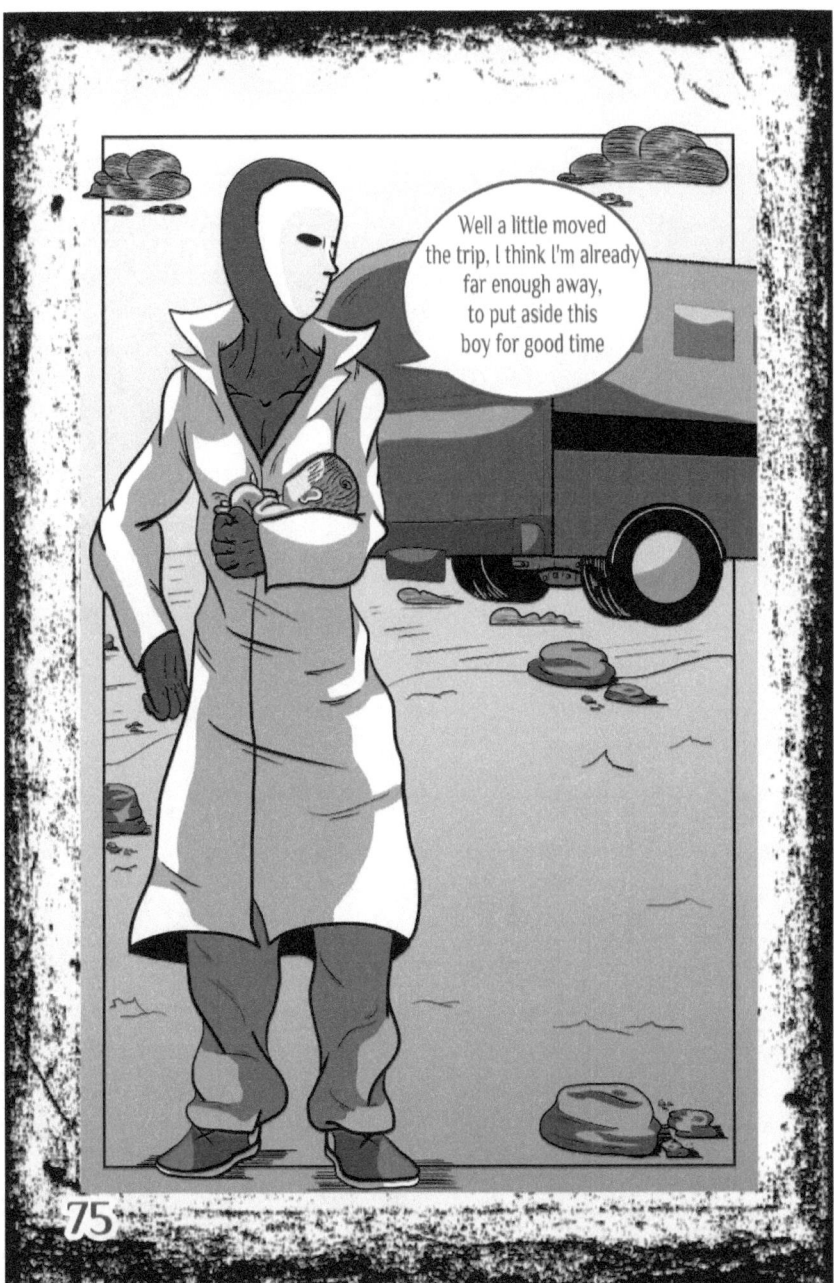

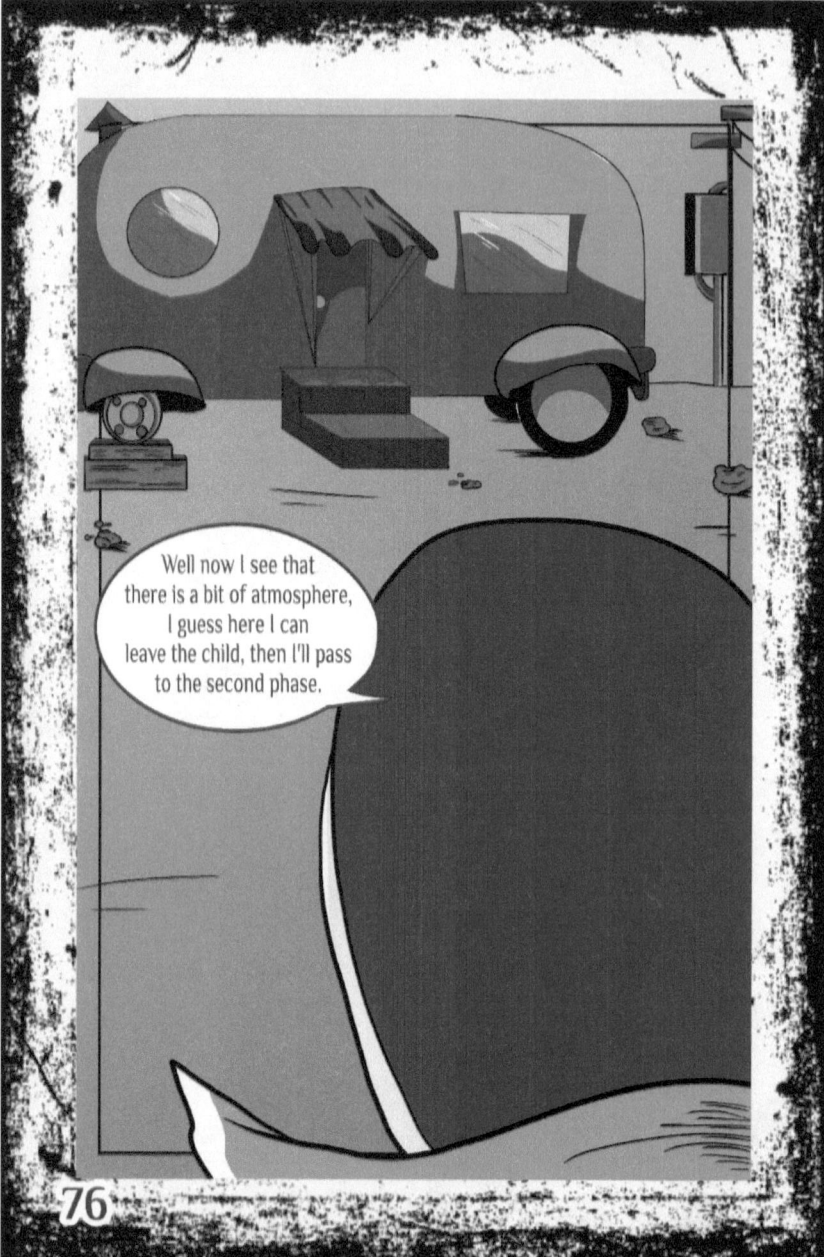

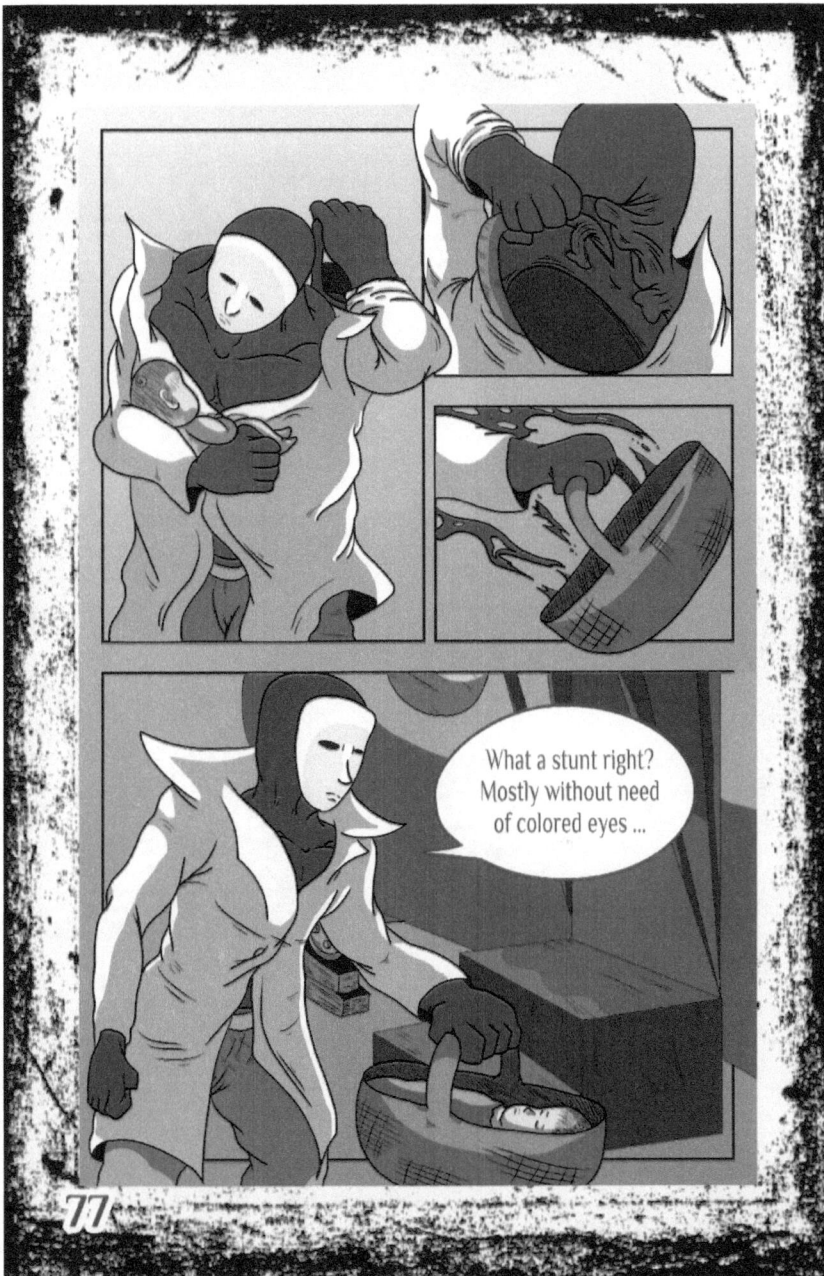

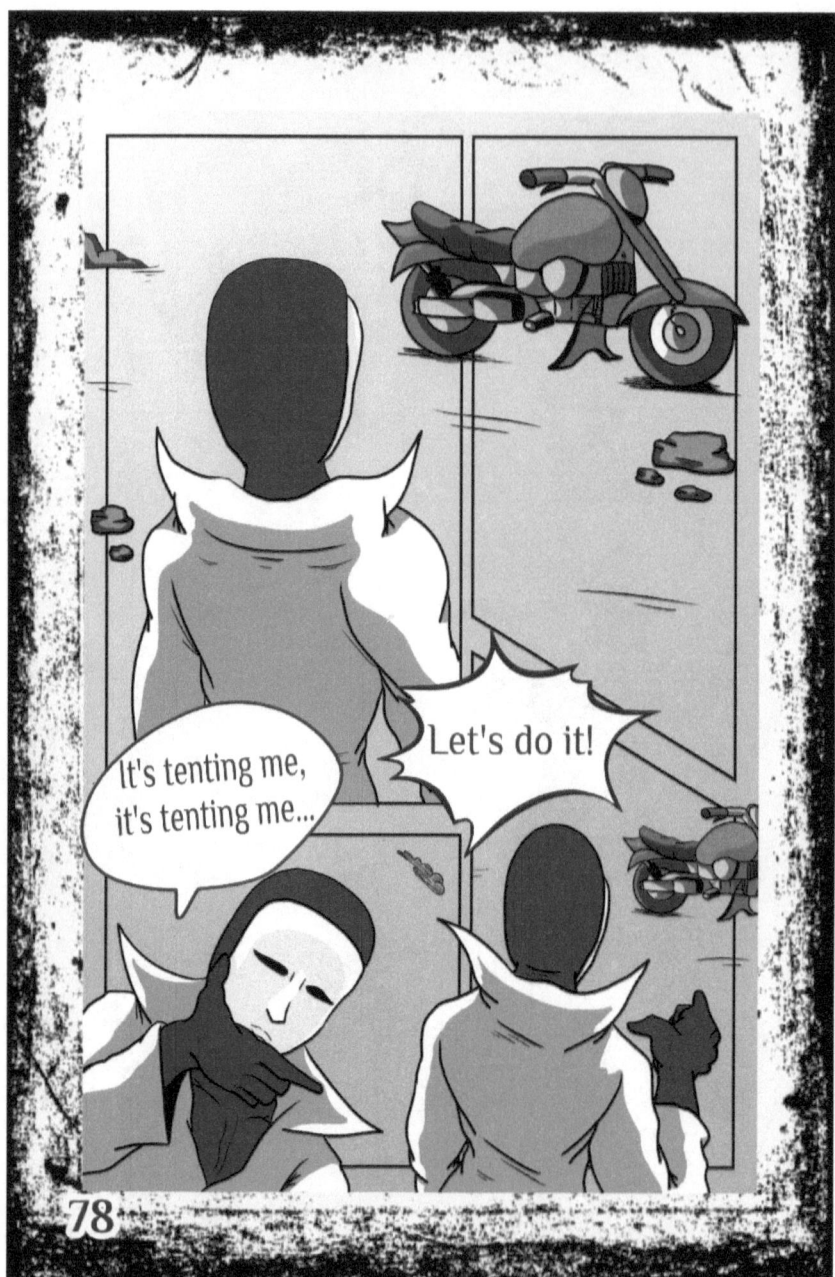

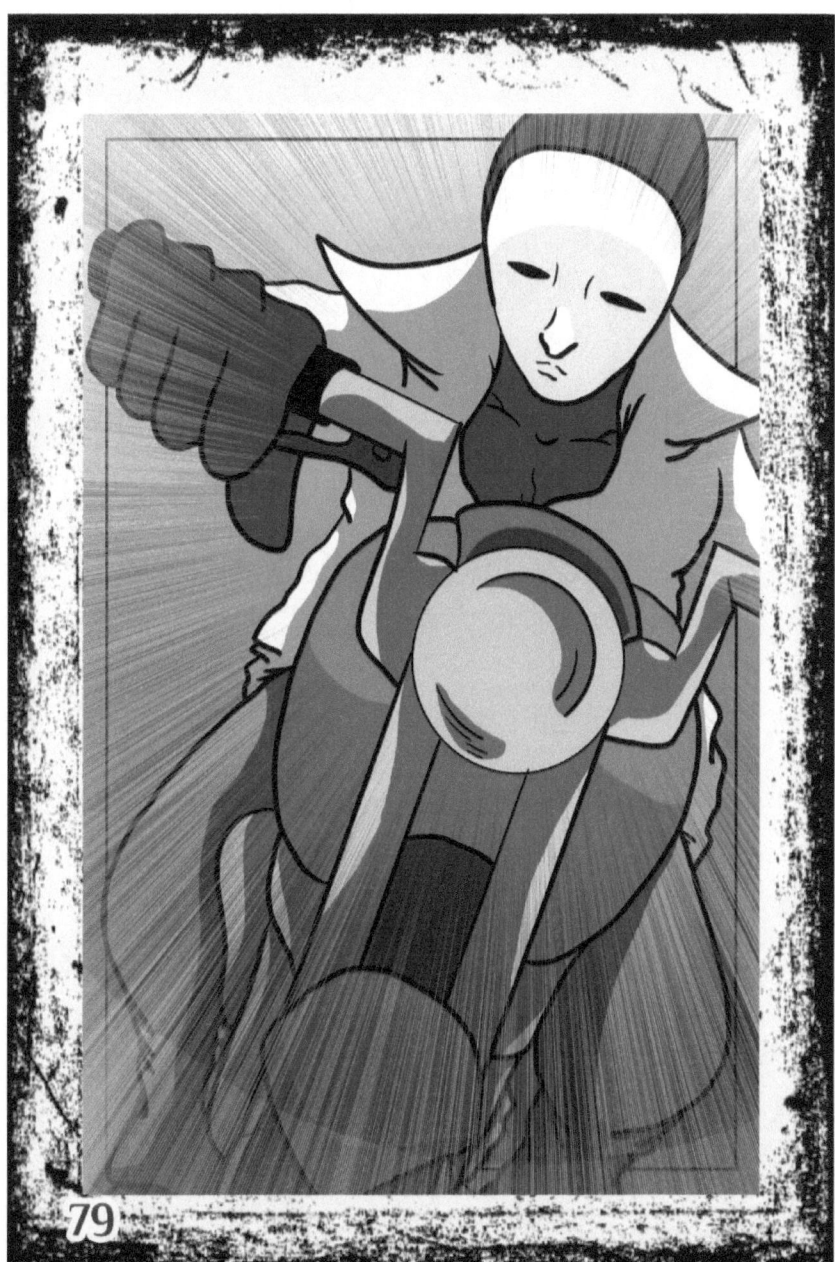

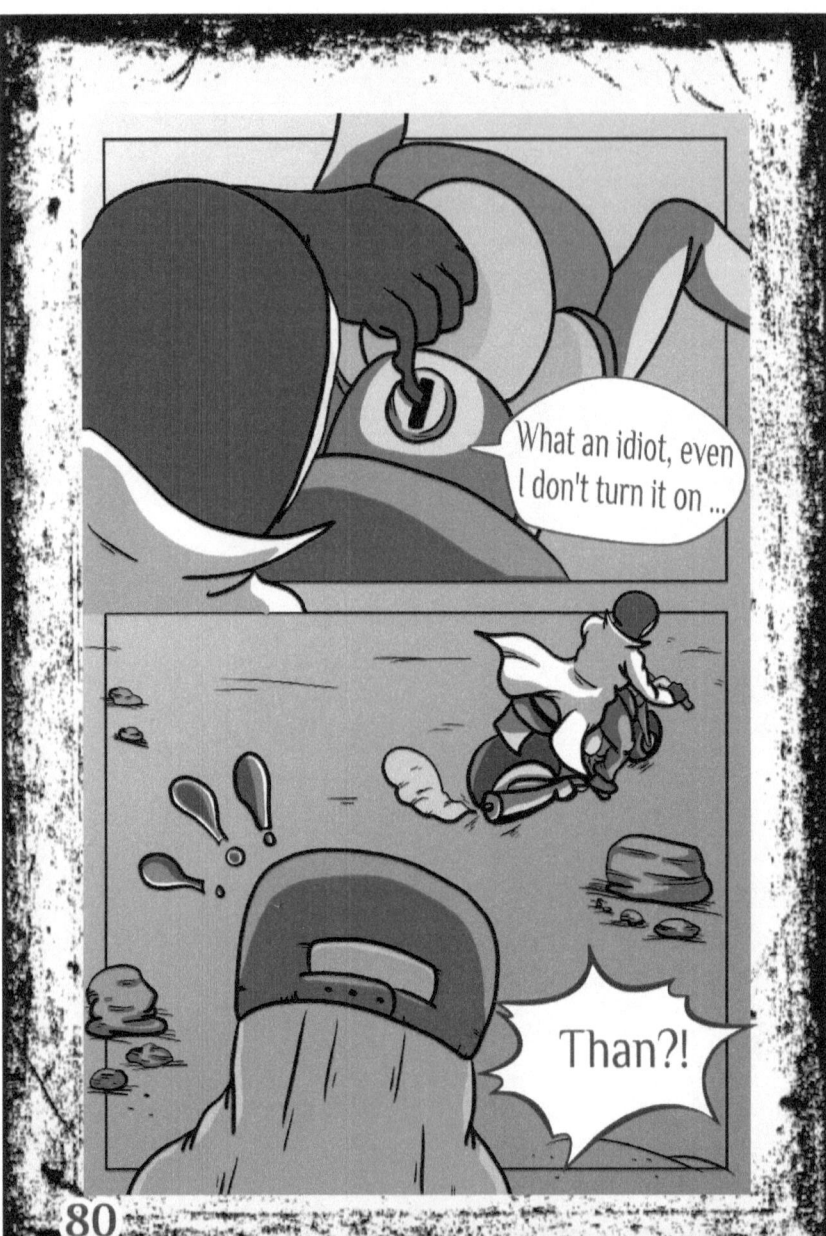

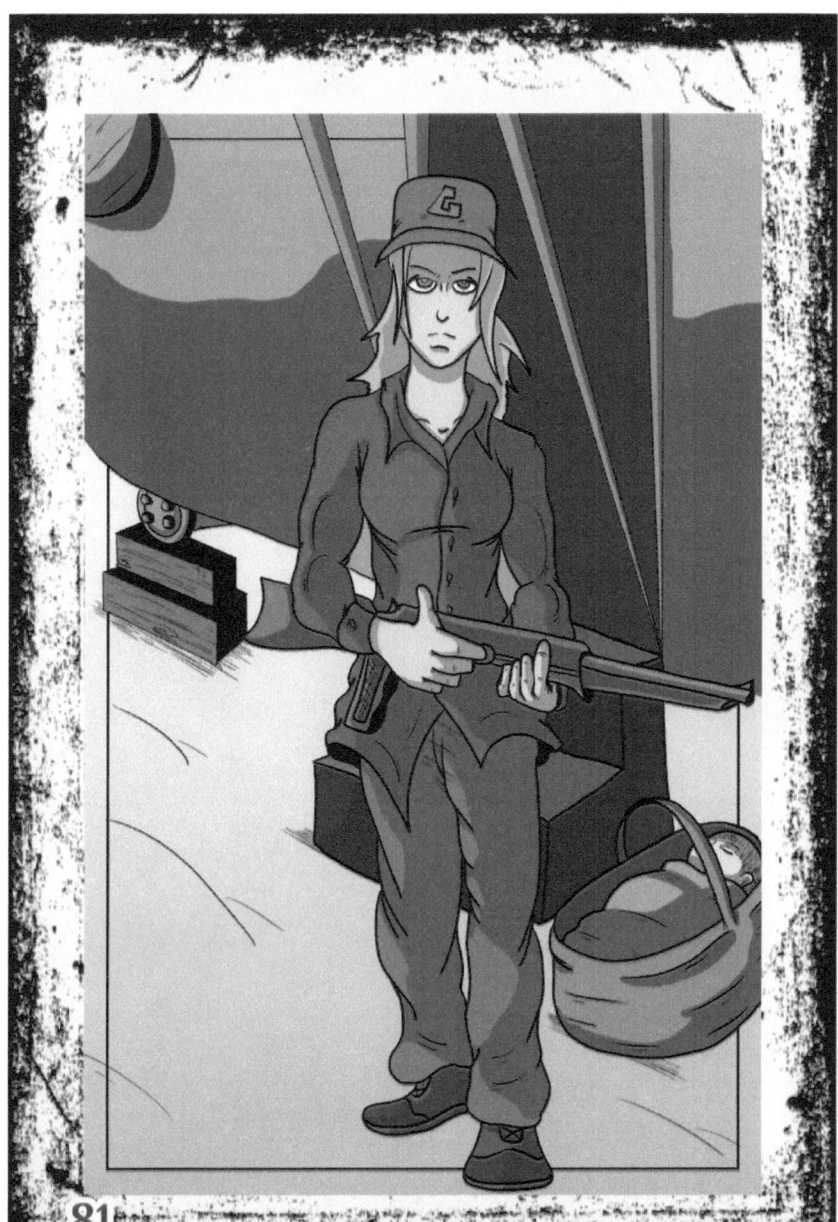

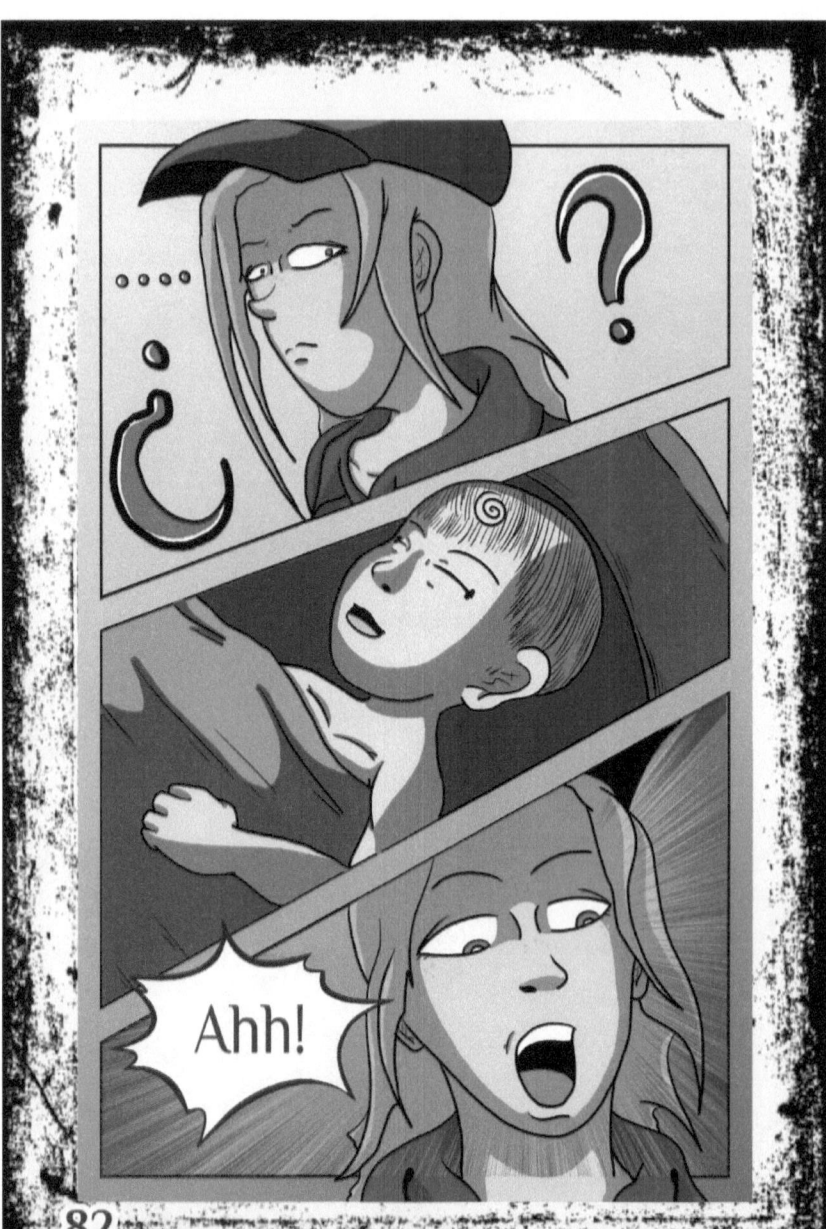

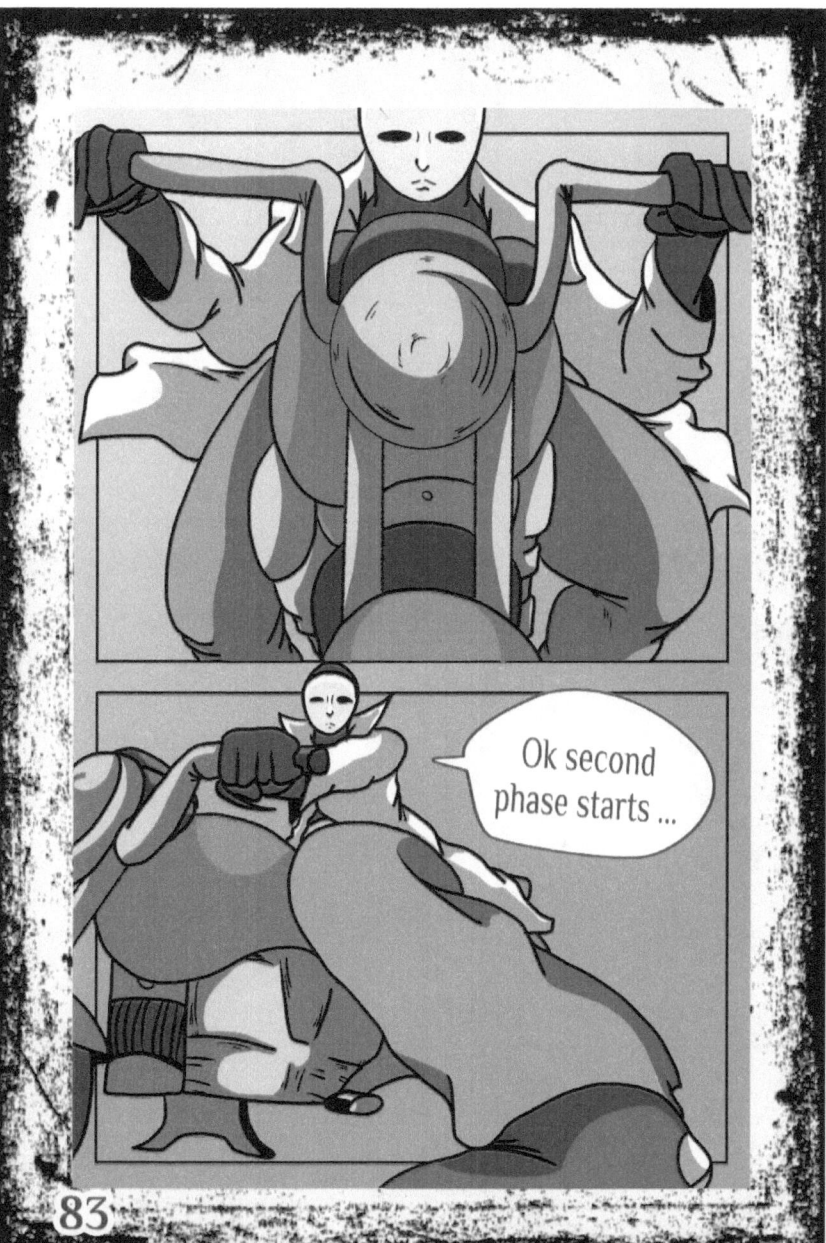

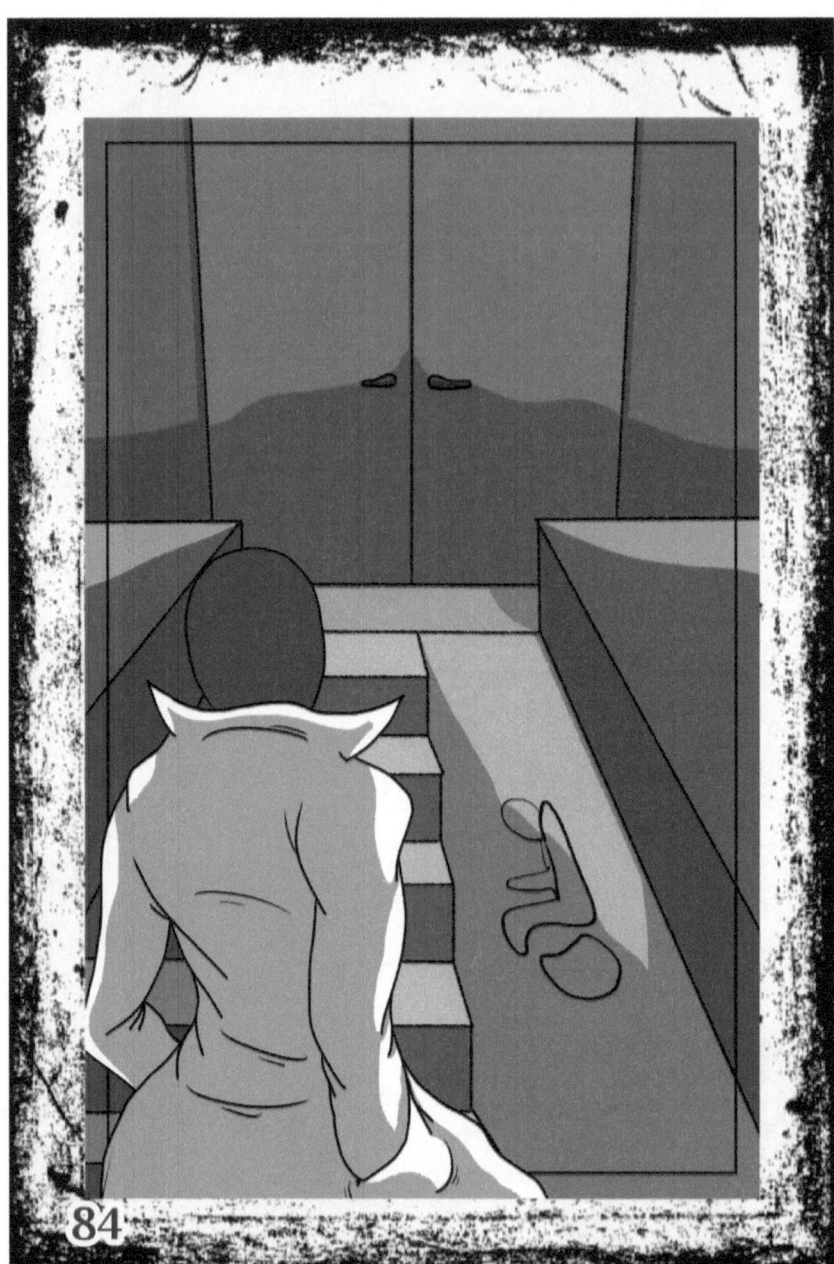

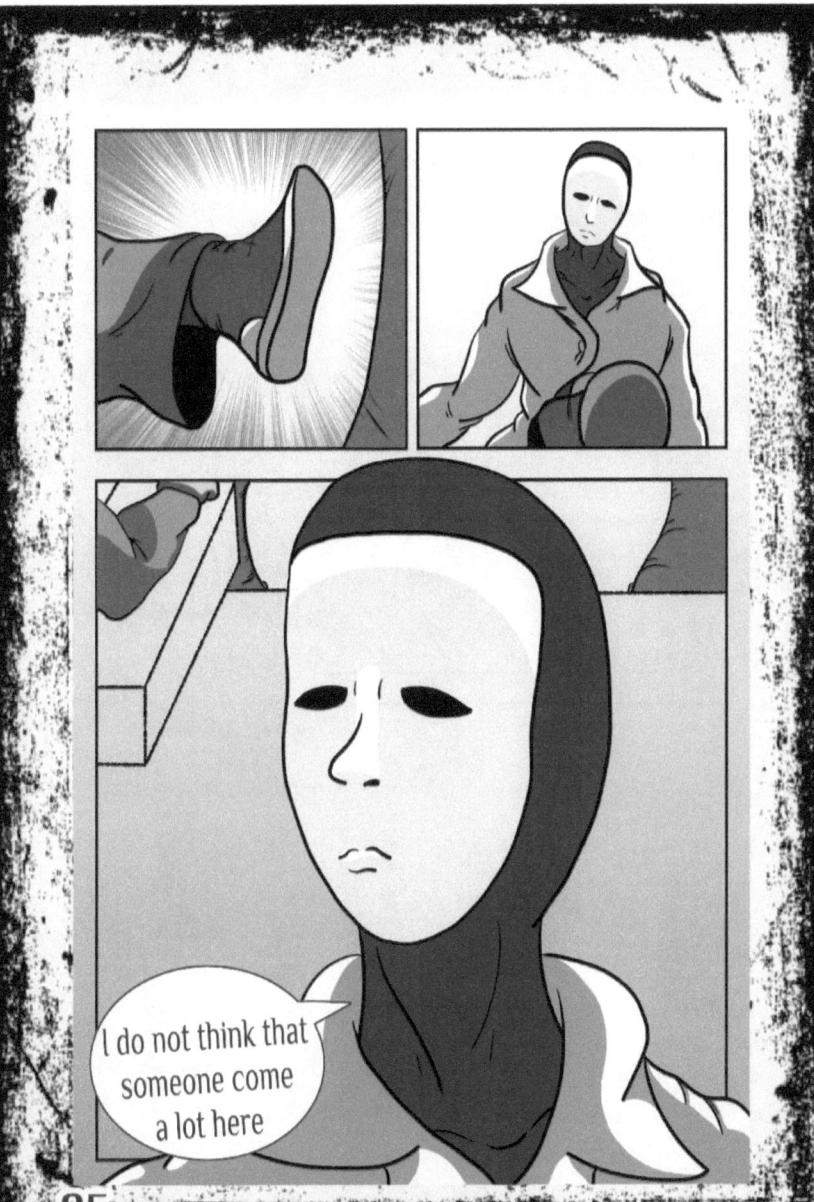

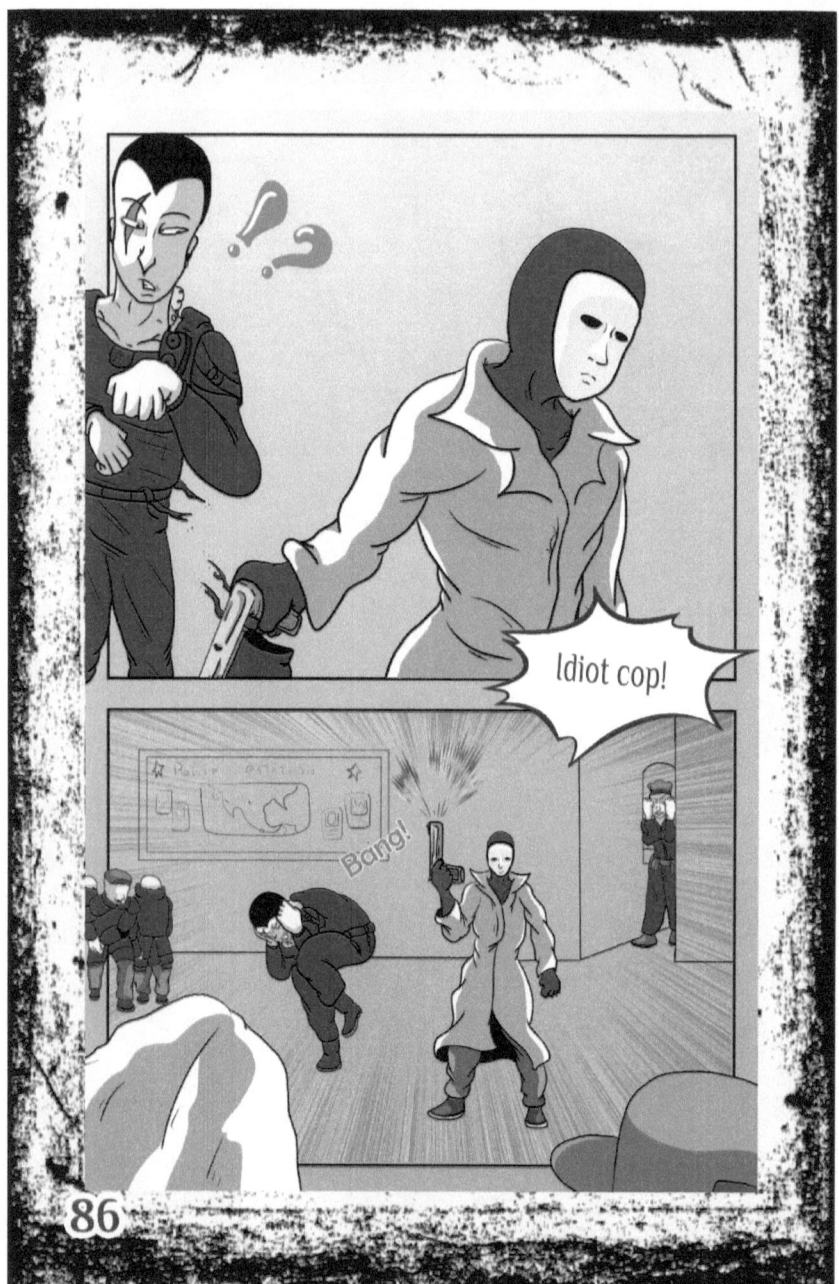

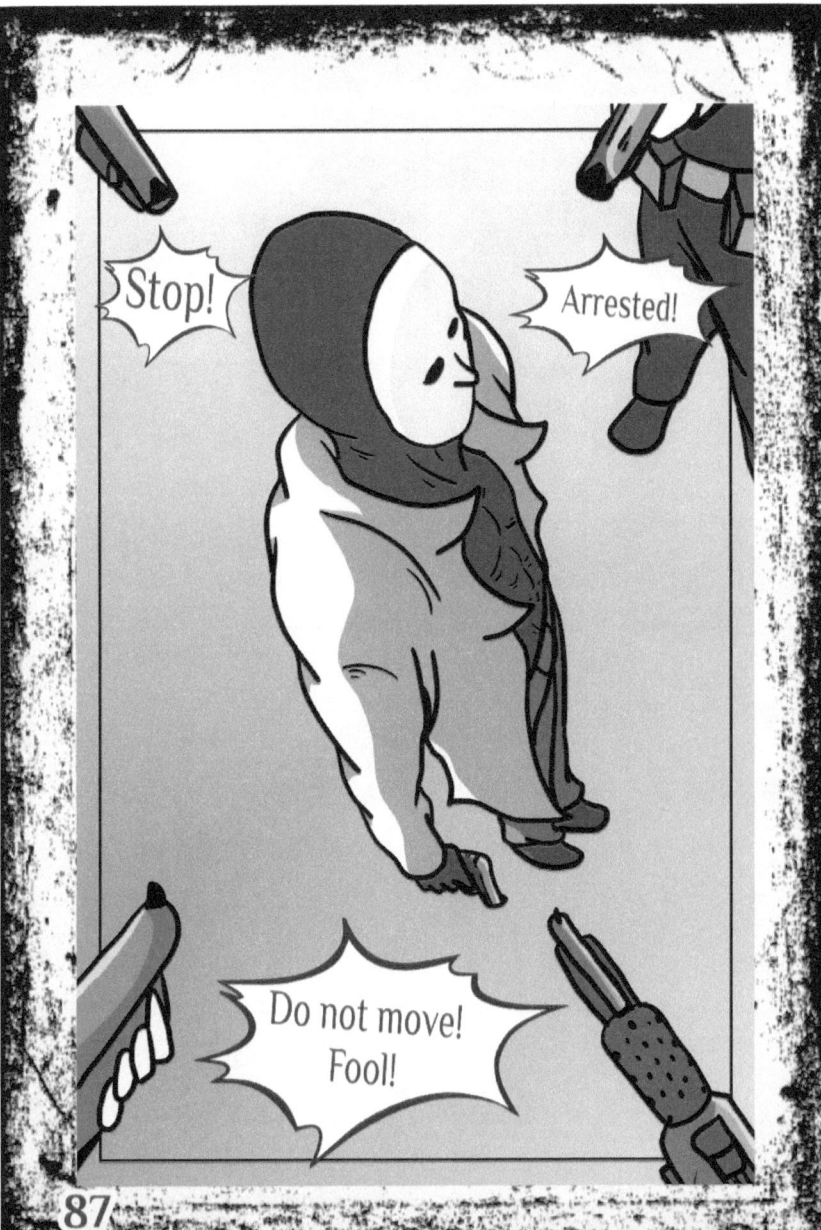

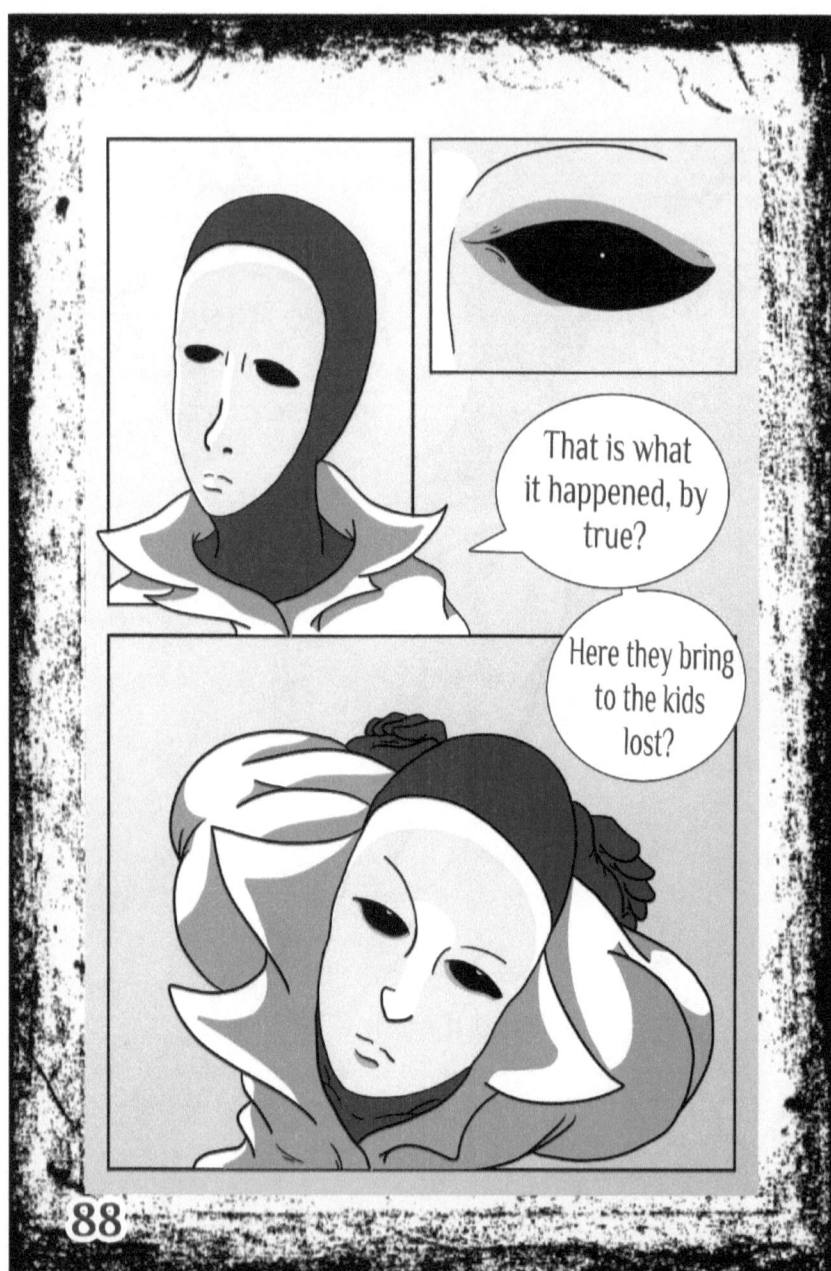

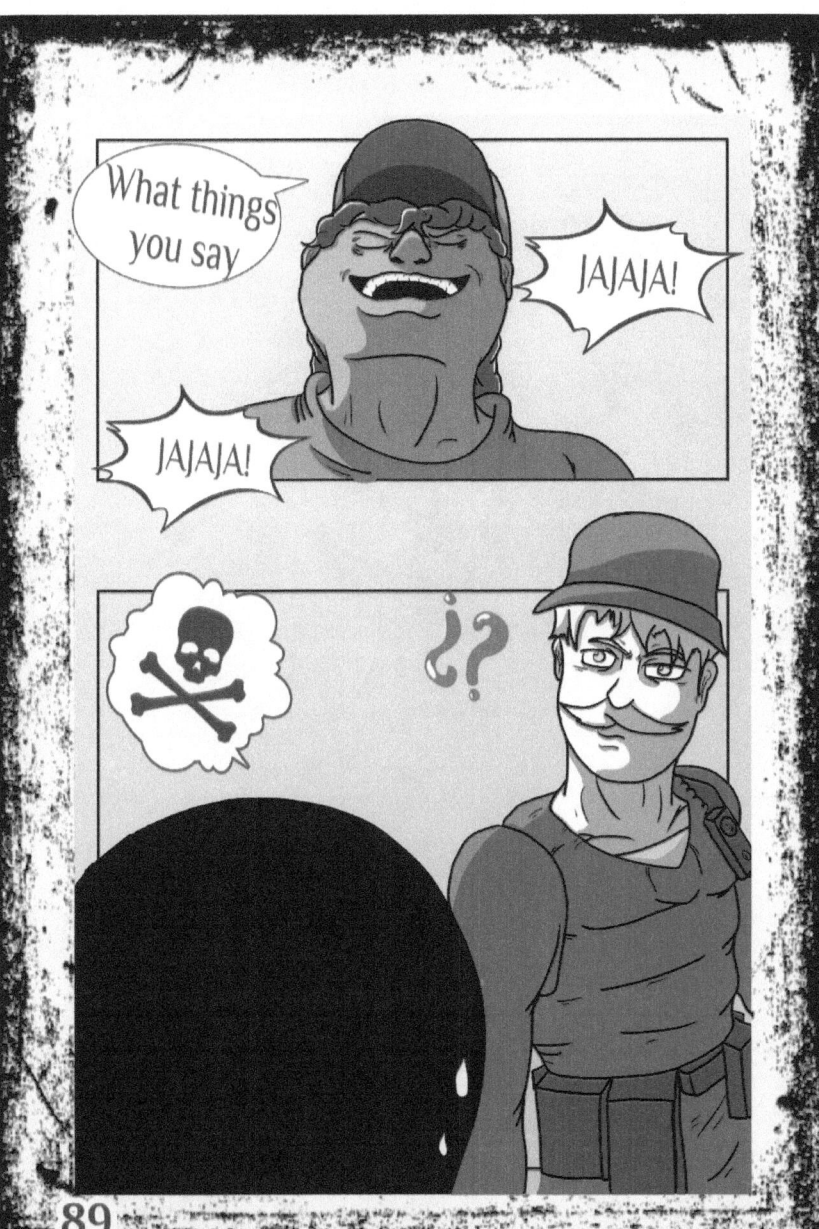

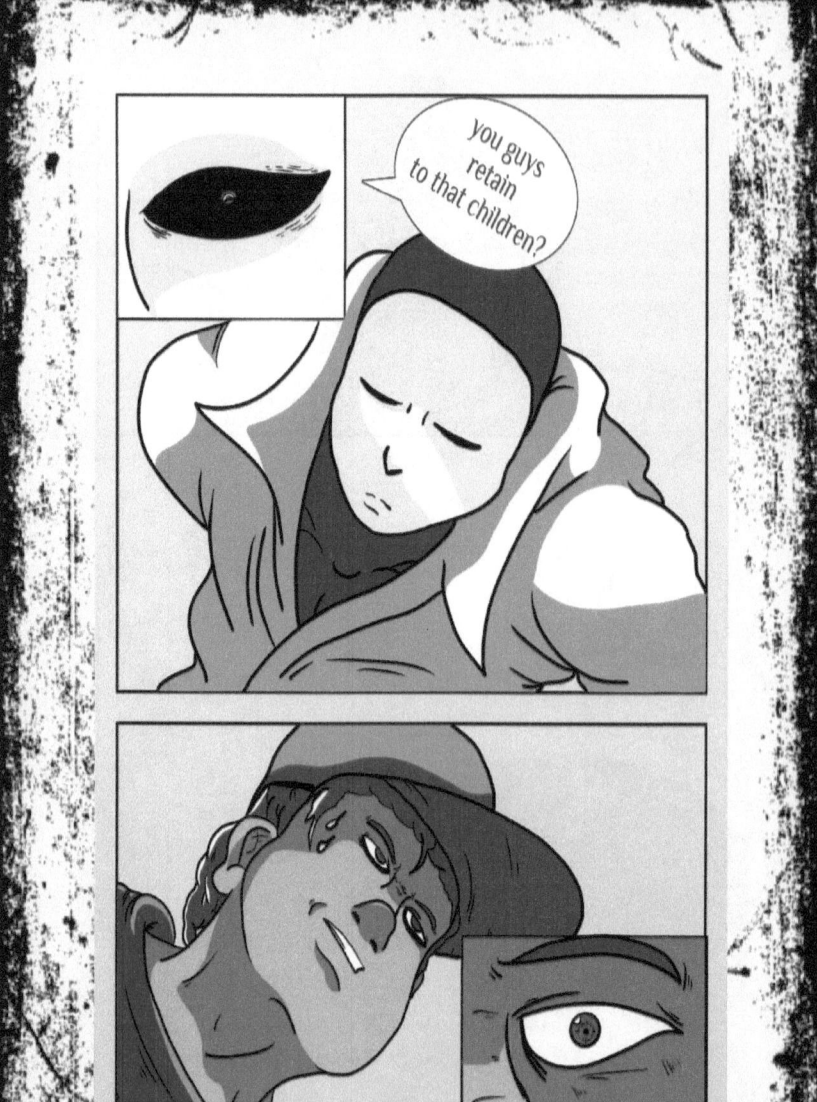

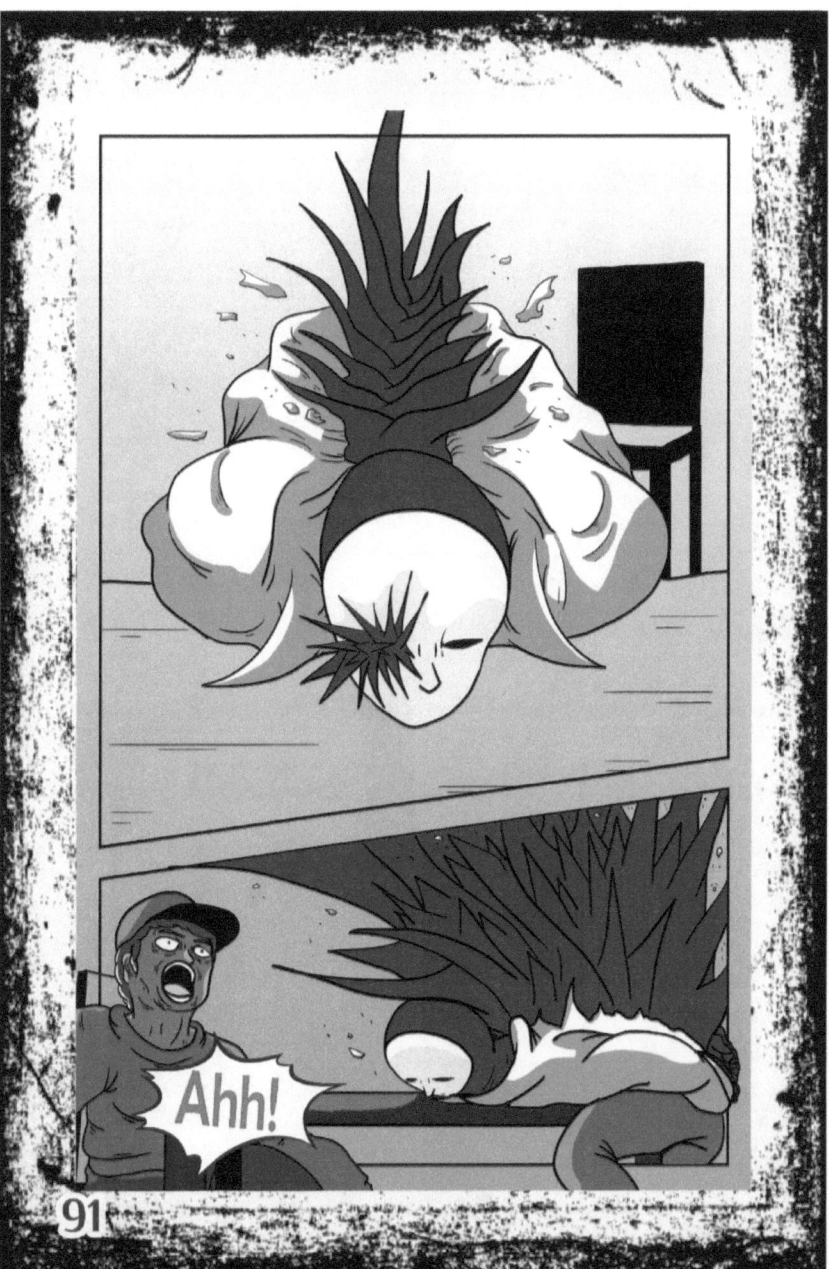

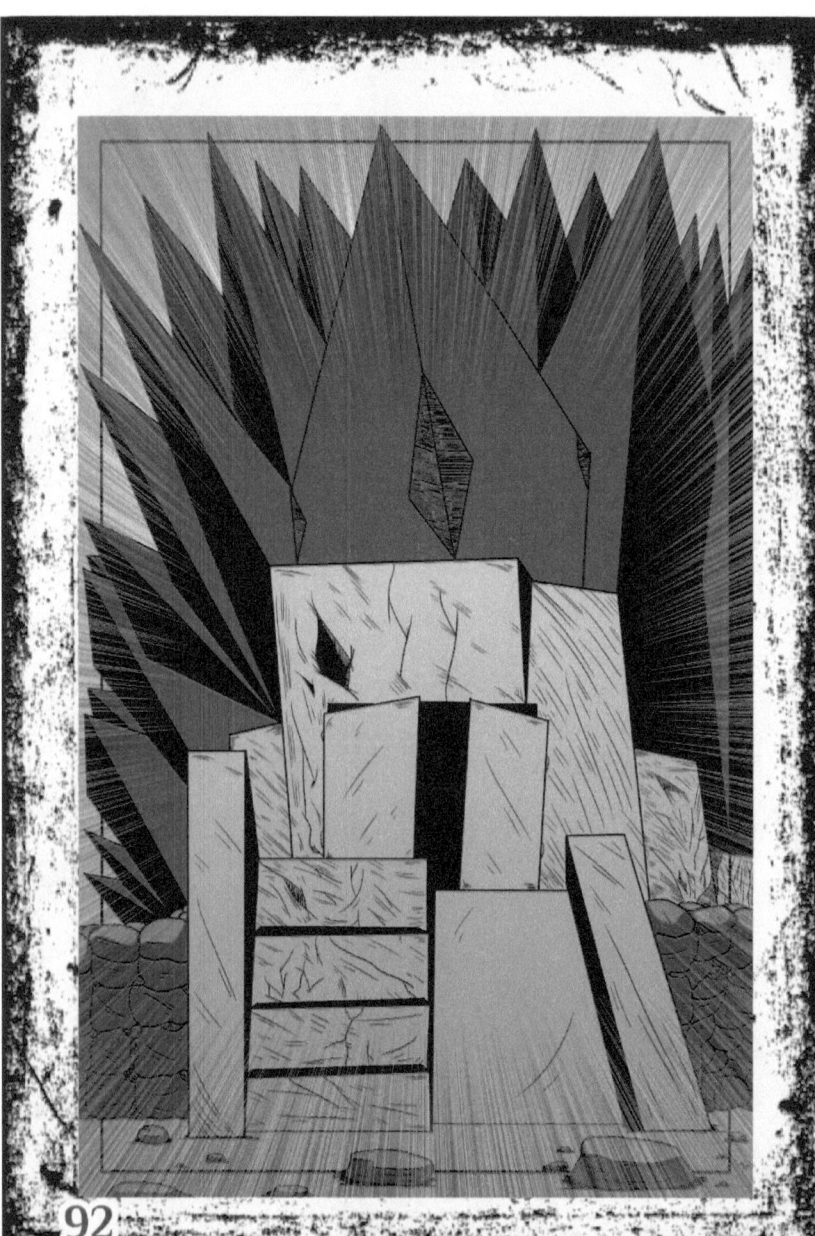

92

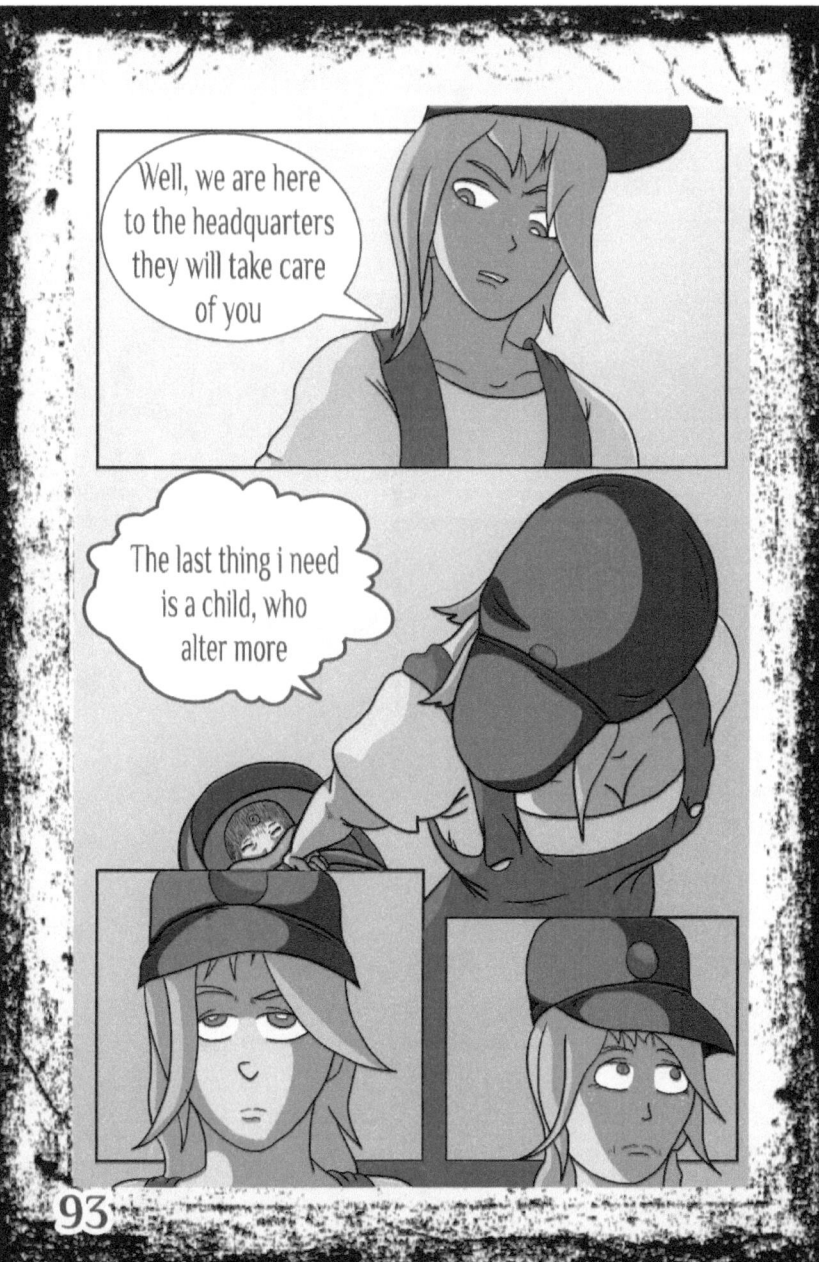

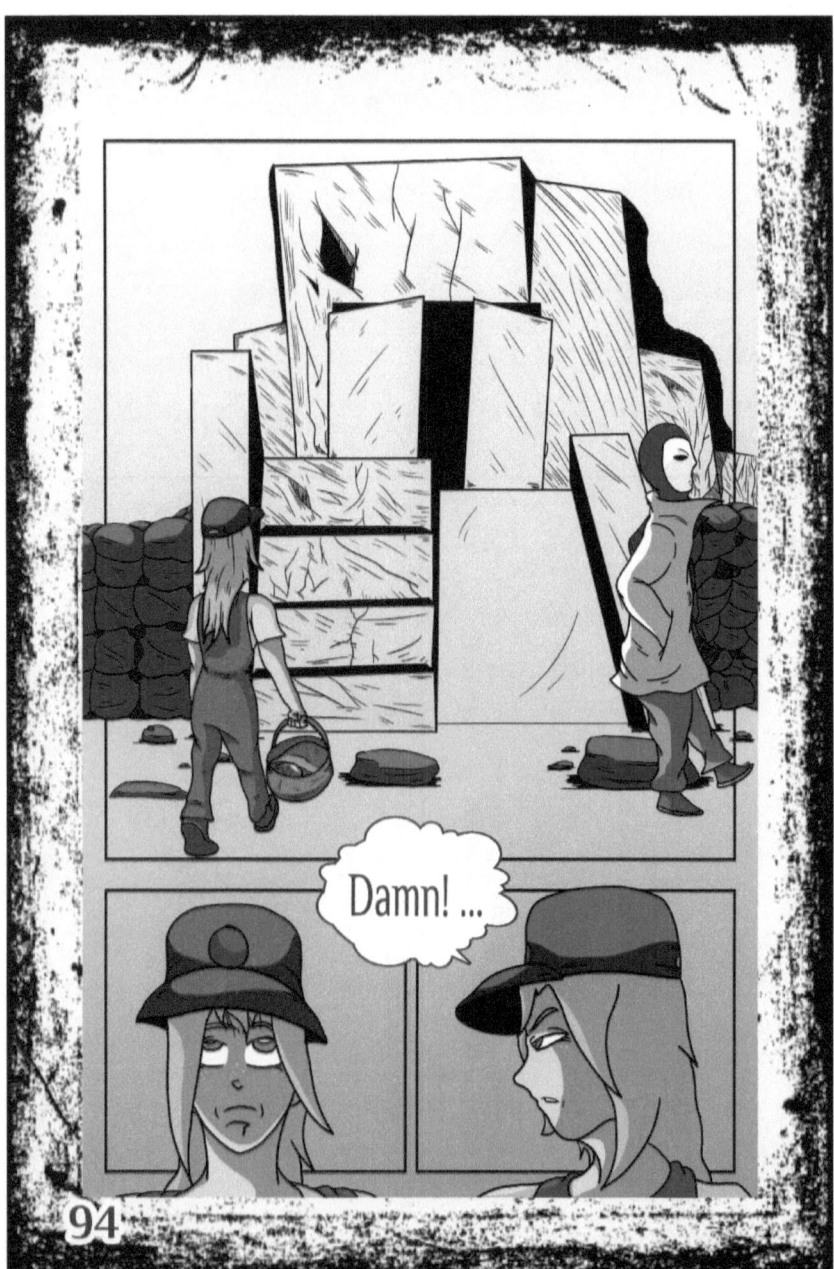

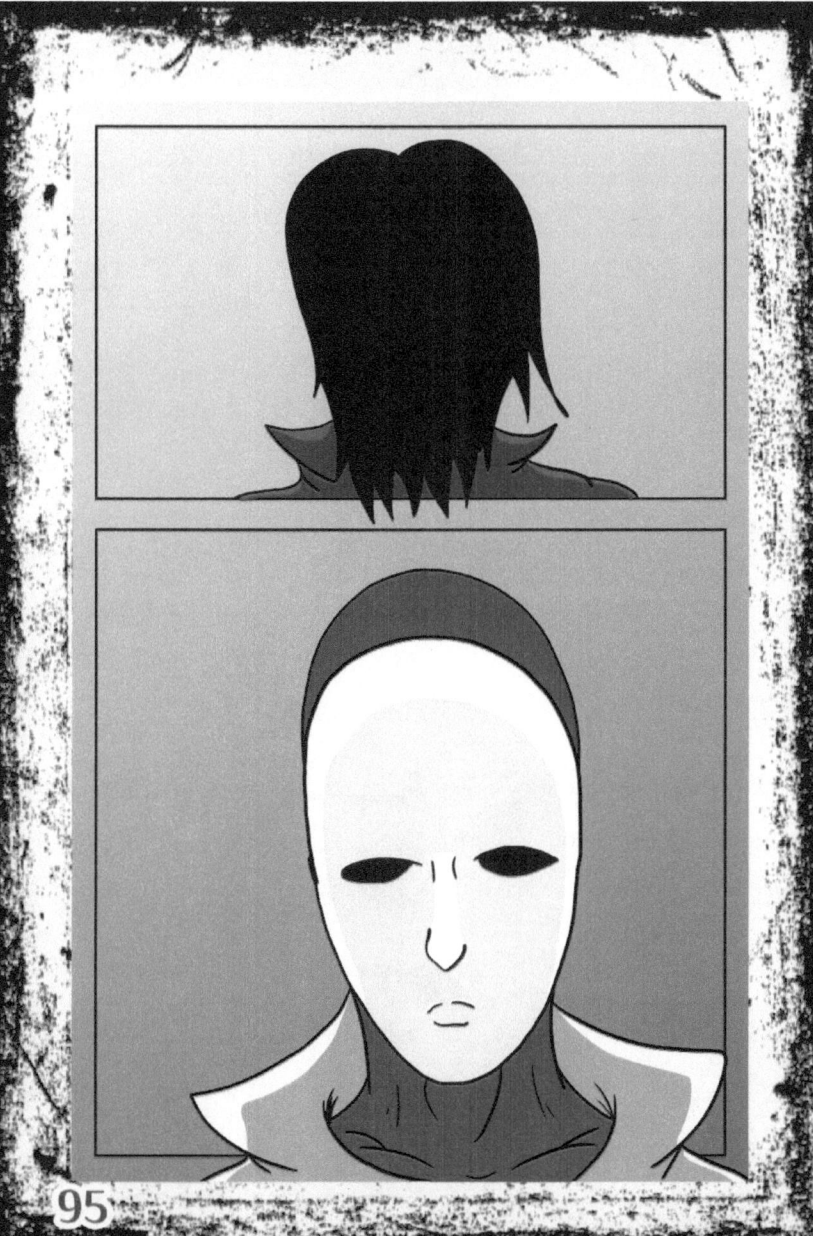

95

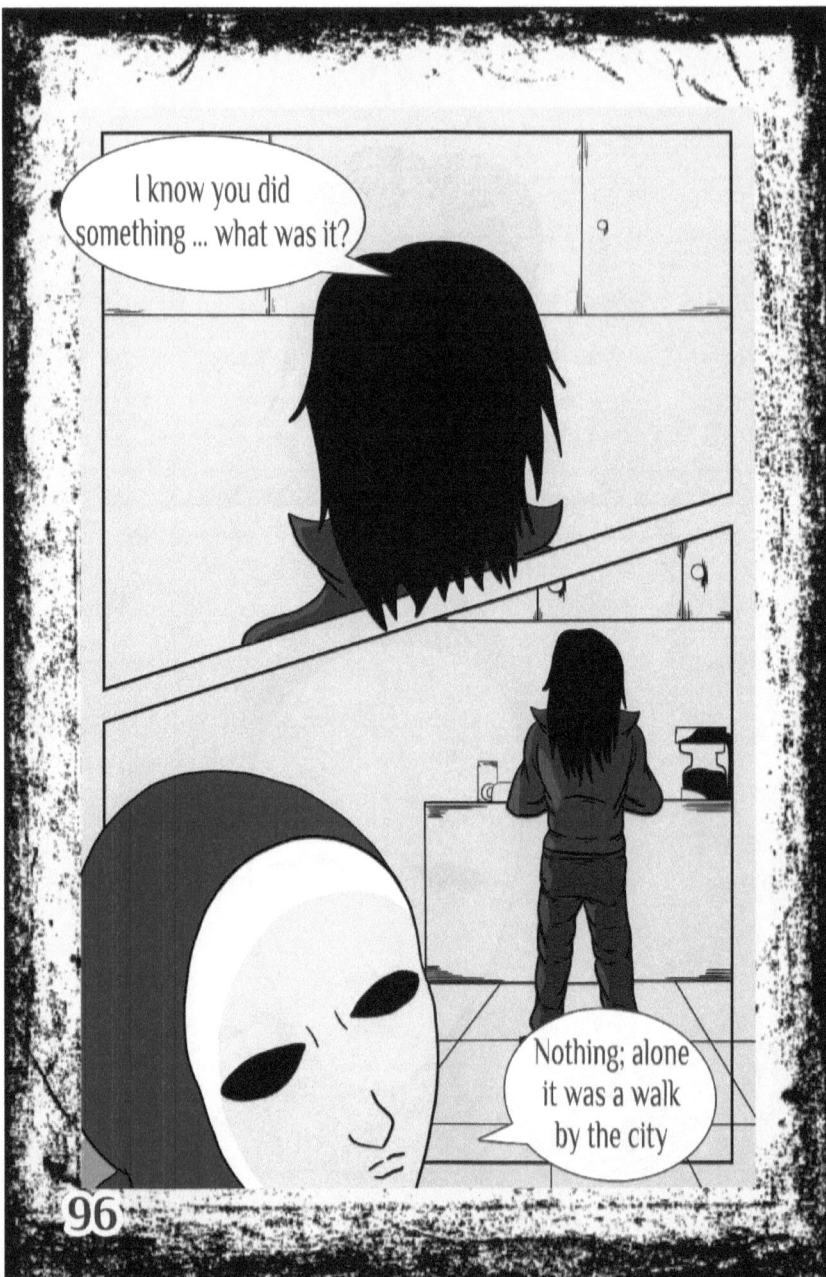

96

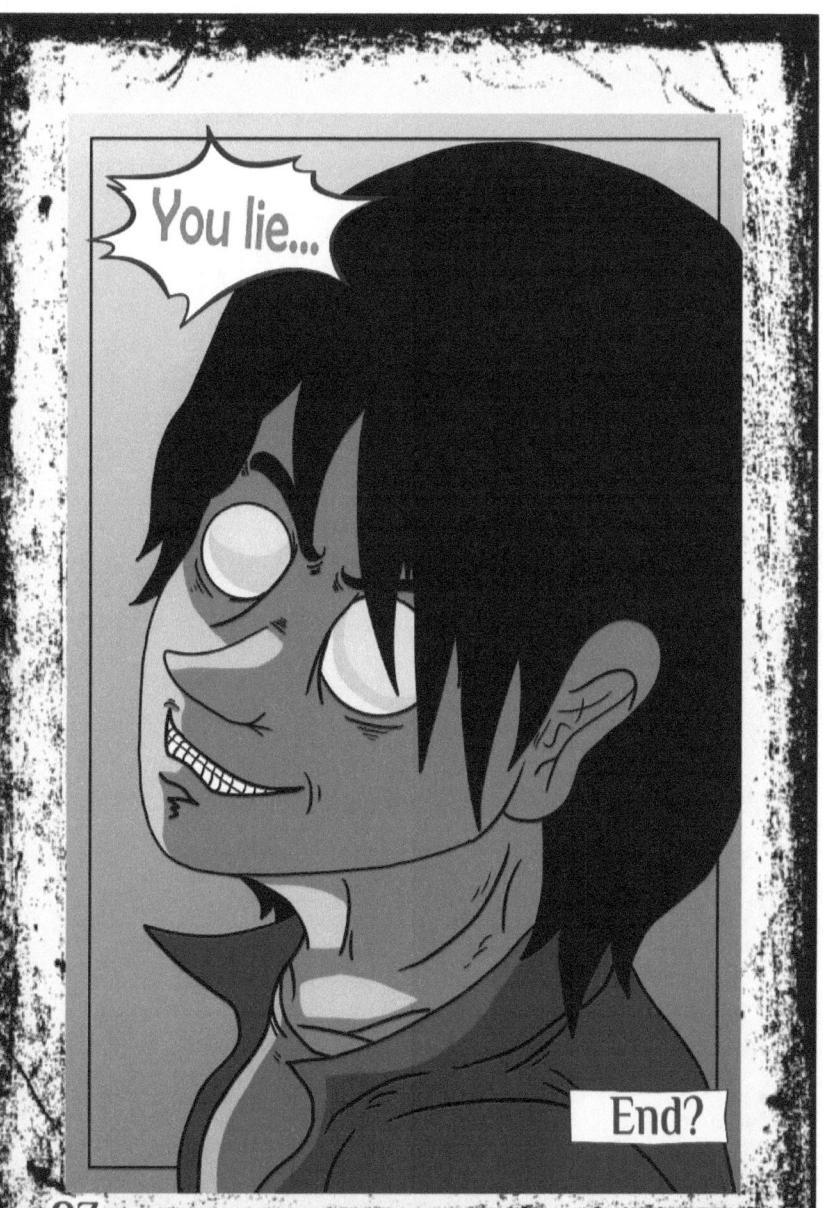

By Tobispartan (Leonardo Gudiño)

ZONE BLACK
All Eye On Me

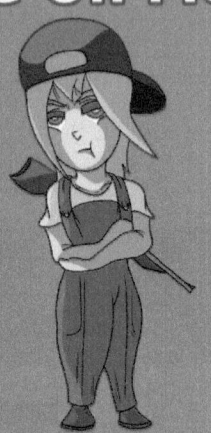

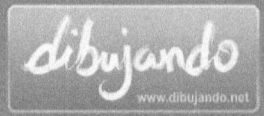

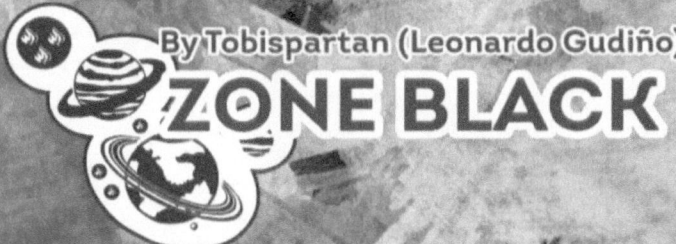

By Tobispartan (Leonardo Gudiño)

ZONE BLACK

Drawing Manual
Lifestyles